To Louise & Ev —
Thanks for your
friendship!
Vicki Hesterman

Environmental Awareness
for Caring People

The EARTH is the LORD'S:
Handle with Care

edited by
Vicki Hesterman

Vicki Hesterman

Accord
Publishing House

FOREWORD

by Dr. Robert Schuller

Our amazing planet is showing serious signs of wear and tear. We have taken our earthly home for granted for too long, and now it's time to give it more attention. It's not too late, though, to stop the slide towards self-destruction.

By thinking and acting positively in small ways, it is possible to make a big difference. Buying recycled goods; keeping our cars well-tuned; using real plates and cups, and conserving water when we shower are just a few things we can do.

The Earth is the Lord's: Handle with Care is an inspiring and practical guide to good stewardship of the earth and its resources. Editor Vicki Hesterman has included essays by Christians of various backgrounds and denominations who have this in common: their love for the Lord and their concern for His handiwork.

We do not have to choose between eternal salvation and earthly responsiblities; it is possible to be an environmentally active and aware evangelical Christian. In fact, taking good care of God's green earth is a beautiful way to show love and respect for our Creator.

October 1990
Garden Grove, California

*The earth is the Lord's and the fulness thereof,
the world, and they that dwell therein.*

*For He hath founded it upon the seas,
and established it upon the floods.*

Psalm 24: 1-2

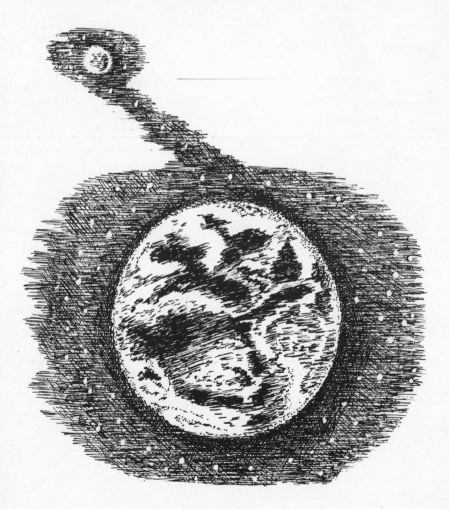

An Observation from the Moon

by Col. James Irwin

As a member of the Apollo 15 crew, I was honored with the rare privilege of walking the surface of the moon. That experience left me with a number of permanent impressions: First, I came to realize in a new way how great God is and how small man is. I also developed a new understanding of the significance of our wonderful planet, Earth, and how privileged man is to inhabit such a realm touched in a special way by the loving hand of our Creator.

I was also impressed by the fact that God has entrusted us with the care and keeping of the earth and its resources—and how in many ways we have failed in this responsibility. We have not been good stewards, and our planet is showing it...

Used by permission of the Christian Nature Federation. See page 102.

The EARTH is the LORD'S:
Handle with Care

Editing and Photography
Vicki Hesterman

Illustrations
Phyllis Hesterman

Cover Design
Sue Hurst and Phyllis Hesterman

"Just for Kids" illustrations by Laura, Andrew and Daniel Hurst
Photo on page 78 by I. K. Cordes

Scripture refererences taken from the following translations:
--The Holy Bible, King James Version.
--The Holy Bible, New International Version. Copyright 1973, 1978, by the International Bible Society. Used by permission.
--The New King James Version. Copyright 1979, 1980, 1982, Thomas Nelson, Inc. , Publishers.
Illustrated account of creation from Genesis 1 and 2.

Accord Publishing House
P.O. Box 582
Napoleon, Ohio 43545
(419) 267-3367

ISBN 0-9628007-0-8
Library of Congress Cataloging Number: 90-84823

*This book is printed on recycled paper
by Thomson-Shore Printers.
10% of the proceeds will be donated to help heal the earth.*

CONTENTS

PART FOUR
Who Can You Call?
What Should You Read?
Where Do You Write?

INTRODUCTION

Earth Day 1990 spawned colorful t-shirts, environmental lectures and dire predictions that the end is near. Although we can't waste any more time in literally cleaning up our act, things are not beyond hope. This book is a call to action for all the Lord's people to actively work to heal the earth.

Thousands of Christians across the country have been quietly environmentally aware for years, many of them long before that first Earth Day in 1970. Stewardship of the earth's resources is part of their Christian value system; keeping the landscape clean is as natural as breathing.

Many believers have kept a distance from the recent secular environmental movement, though, preferring not to be aligned with groups that worship nature or espouse abortion as a means of population control. Some avoid action because of their belief that redemption and salvation are more important than recycling and conservation. Not only New Agers and old hippies should show concern about the health of the planet, though.

We can simultaneously conserve water and grow spiritually. We don't have to align ourselves with groups whose philosophies are incompatible with ours. We don't have to choose between salvation and environmental activism. We do, however, have a moral obligation to future generations to care for our earthly heritage.

It takes time, energy and commitment to be environmentally responsible. We live in a fast-food, quick-trip, one-stop-shop society. It's easiest to use disposable diapers and paper plates. It's faster to dump discards at the landfill than to sort them for recycling. Time will test the commitment of the new environmental activists and separate the truly dedicated from the terminally trendy.

This is not a simple issue; there are trade-offs. Saving northern California forests and owls puts hundreds of people out of work. Most recycled paper and biodegradable detergents are more expensive than less earth-friendly products. Collecting and sorting cans, bottles and newspapers takes precious time.

Working on this project has changed some of my own habits. I'm still far from perfect, but I've accepted the wisdom of *precycling*; I recycle glass, aluminum and paper; I walk more and drive less. I never did wash my car much, but now I have a good excuse—I'm conserving water and energy.

The Christians who contributed to this book come from various professions and philosophical persuasions. Lutherans, Baptists, Methodists, Nazarenes, Presbyterians and non-denominational believers have joined in this appeal for awareness and action.

Part One is a dedication to the Creator of the earth and all life. In it, relevant Scriptures, the Genesis account, and illustrations celebrate creation.

Part Two is a brief synopsis of helpful hints, gleaned from pamphlets, articles, books, lectures, and personal interviews. A special illustrated "Just for Kids" section is designed for children from ages 6-11.

In Part Three, Christians of various backgrounds write about their experiences and opinions on creation and environmental responsibility. Part Four lists books, magazines and environmental action groups, but is not intended to be an exhaustive list of resources. More literature on the subject is available in bookstores, libraries, churches, and other stores.

If this book sparks a desire in the reader to start a recycling bin at work, to organize a Sunday School tree-planting outing, or to pray for the continued healing of our world, this labor of love will have been worth the time it required.

Christians today cannot ignore the call to be at the forefront of the environmental movement. Some have heard that call and are already there.

Vicki Hesterman
San Diego, 1990

Part One

Why We Should Take Care of the Earth

Lord,
You have been our dwelling place
in all generations.

Before the mountains were brought forth
or ever you had formed the earth and the world

Even from everlasting to everlasting
You are God.

Psalm 90:1-2

The following creation account is
from Genesis 1 and 2.

In the beginning

God created the heavens

and the earth.

The earth was without form or void;

darkness was

on the face

of the deep.

And the Spirit of God was hovering

over the face of the waters.

Then God said,

"Let there be Light."

The heavens declare the glory of God;
the skies proclaim the work of his hand.
Psalm 19:1

Praise the Lord.
Praise God in his sanctuary;
praise him in his mighty heavens.
Psalm 150:1-2

Those who are wise will shine
like the brightness of the heavens,
and those who lead many to righteousness
like the stars
for ever and ever.
Daniel 12:3

Let there be a firmament

in the midst

of the waters.

and let it divide

the waters

from

the waters

and **G**od called

the firmament

Heaven.

The earth is the Lord's and the fulness thereof,
the world, and they that dwell therein.

For he hath founded it upon the seas,
and established it upon the floods.
Psalm 24:1-2

He causes the grass to grow for the cattle
and the vegetation for the service of man,
that he may bring forth food out of the earth.
Psalm 104:14

So neither he who plants
nor he who waters is anything,
but only God, who makes things grow.
I Corinthians 3:7

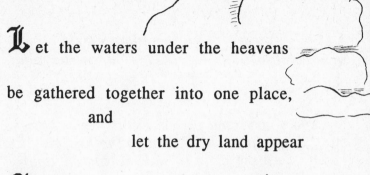

L et the waters under the heavens

be gathered together into one place,
and

let the dry land appear

A nd God called the dry land E arth . . .

and the waters S eas.

T hen God said,

L et the earth bring forth grass,

the herb that yields seed, and the fruit tree

that yields fruit according to its kind,

whose seed is in itself.

To everything there is a season
and a time to every purpose under heaven.
Ecclesiastes 3:1

Every good and perfect gift is from above,
coming down from the Father of the heavenly lights,
who does not change like shifting shadows.
James 1: 17-18

The day is yours,
and yours also is the night;
You established the sun and the moon.
It was you who set the boundaries of the earth;
You made both summer and winter.
Psalm 74:16-17

Praise the Lord.
Praise the Lord from the heavens,
praise him in the heights above.
Praise him all his angels,
praise him all his heavenly hosts.
Praise him, sun and moon,
praise him all you shining stars.
Praise him, you highest heavens
and you waters above the skies.
Let them praise the name of the Lord
for He commanded and they were created.
Psalm 148:1-5

Let there be lights

in the firmament of the heavens

to divide the day

from the night

and let them be for signs and seasons,

and for days and years,

and let them be for lights in the

firmament of the heavens to give

light on the earth . . . the greater light

to rule the day

and the lesser light

to rule the night.

He made the stars also.

Oh, Lord, how manifold are they work!
in wisdom hast thou made them all:
the earth is full of thy riches.

So is this great and wide sea,
wherein are things creeping innumerable,
both small and great beasts...

There is that leviathan,
whom thou hast made to play therein.
Psalm 104:24-26

Look at the birds of the air.

Do not worry about your life,
what you will eat or what you will drink,
nor about your body, what you will put on.

Is not life more than food
and the body more than clothing?
Matthew 6:26

𝕷et the waters abound

      with an abundance

           of living creatures

and

    let birds fly above the earth

        across the firmament of the heavens.

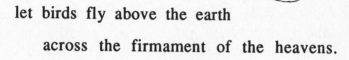

So

      God created the great sea creatures

and every living thing that moves,

      with which the waters abounded,

        according to their kind

and every winged bird

      according to its kind.

𝕬nd God said, Be fruitful and multiply

    and fill the waters in the seas,

    and let the birds multiply on earth.

What is man, that thou art mindful of him?
and the son of man, that thou visitest him?
For thou hast made him a little lower than the angels,
and hast crowned him with glory and honor.
Thou madest him to have dominion
over the works of thy hands;
thou hast put all things under his feet.
Psalms 8:4-6

Of his own will, he brought us forth
by the word of truth,

that we might be a kind of first fruit
of his creatures.
James 1:18

Neither is there any creature
that is not manifest in his sight:
but all things are naked and opened
unto the eyes of him whom we have to do.
Hebrews 4:13.

Let the earth bring forth living creatures
         according to its kind
Cattle and creeping things
            and beasts of the earth
         according to their kinds.

Then God said,
     Let us make man
     in our own image, after our likeness:
Let them have dominion over
     the fish of the sea,
     the birds of the air,
     the cattle,
     all the earth,
     and every creeping thing
     that creeps on earth.

     So God created man in His own image . . .
male and female . . .
     and blessed them
     and said,

       Be fruitful and multiply
     and fill the earth and subdue it.

Come unto me,
all ye who labor and are heavy laden,
and I will give you rest.

Matthew 11: 28

This is what the Lord says:
Heaven is my throne,
and the earth is my footstool.
Where is the house you will build for me?
And where will my resting place be?

Isaiah 66:1

All the heavens
　　　and the earth
and all the host of them
　　　were finished.

　　　On the seventh day God ended
His work . . . . . .　　　and He rested
　　　from all the work He had done.

Then
　　God blessed the seventh day
　　　　　and sanctified it,
　　because in it He rested
　　　　　from all His work.

Make a joyful noise unto the Lord, all ye lands.

Serve the Lord with gladness:
Come before his presence with singing.

Know ye that the Lord he is God:
it is he that hath made us, and not we ourselves;
We are his people and the sheep of his pasture.

Psalm 100: 1-3

God is our refuge and strength.
A very present help in trouble,
therefore we will not fear,
though the earth be removed
and though the mountains be carried into the sea.

Psalm 46: 1-2

The sun and moon
must shine for us day and night;
the sky
must give us rain, clouds, shade, and dew;
the earth
must give us all kinds of growing things and animals;
the waters
must give us fish and countless necessities;
the air
must supply birds as well as our breath;
fire
must warm us and give us countless benefits.

And who can enumerate everything?
It cannot be otherwise or better expressed
than in these short words:
"Great are the works of the Lord."

And it cannot be sufficiently proclaimed to all eternity,
even though the leaves and grass were all tongues.

--Martin Luther

ALL CREATURES OF OUR GOD AND KING

Written by Francis of Assisi in 1225

All creatures of our God and King
Lift up your voice and with us sing
Lord, we praise You.   Alleluia.
O brother sun with golden beam
O sister moon with silver gleam
O sister water, flowing clear,
Make music for thy Lord to hear.
O brother fire who lights the night
Providing warmth, enhancing sight.
Dear mother earth who day by day
Unfolded blessings on our way,
The flowers and fruits that in thee grow
Let them God's glory also show.
Let all things their Creator bless
And worship him in humbleness,
Praise, praise the Father, praise the Son
and praise the Spirit, Three in One.
O praise Him.   Alleluia.   Alleluia.

Part Two

How We Can
Take Care of
the Earth

FOR THE BEAUTY OF THE EARTH

written by Folliot S. Pierpoint in 1864.

For the beauty of the earth
For the glory of the skies
For the love which from our birth
Over and around us lies.

For the beauty of each hour
Of the day and of the night
Hill and vale and tree and flower
Sun and moon and stars of light

For the joy of ear and eye
For the heart and mind's delight
For the mystic harmony
Linking sense to sound and sight

For thyself, best gift divine
To the world so freely given
For that great, great love of thine
Peace on earth and joy in heaven

Lord of all, to thee we raise
This our hymn of grateful praise.

TREES, PLEASE

1. Recycle newspapers at home, at school and at work. Call your city or county offices for the nearest recycling centers. Don't wait for someone else to set up a collection bin. Some estimates say that 30-50% of the waste in landfills is paper--much of it newspaper. It takes more than a million trees each week to provide Americans with our newspapers; recycling this paper saves trees and energy.

2. Save white paper from letters, photocopy machines, old tests, office forms, etc. One secretary cuts these sheets up into notepaper; a librarian turns it in for cash to finance a mission trip, and pre-school children love to draw on the clean sides. Nearly all paper and envelopes can be recycled.

3. Contact your favorite magazine and ask them to consider printing the inside text on recycled and recyclable paper. Glossy covers would still protect the product, but recyclable pages would be much better for the environment.   Although glossy paper is difficult to recycle, recyclable glossy paper is being tested.

4. Plant trees whenever possible--on the office grounds, the school grounds, or your own property. Organize and help fund a tree-planting activity. Check with a local nursery to choose hardy, native plants. Trees cool the air (which can reduce global warming) and filter out carbon dioxide. When grown, a tree absorbs 12-15 pounds of carbon dioxide a year. Trees are especially needed in cities, where they can help reduce air conditioner use by 10-50%.

5. Use canvas or net bags when shopping. A bonus: canvas bags don't tear and let eggs fall out to break on the ground. When you do take paper bags, re-use them. Some grocery and drug stores give a slight discount if you bring your own bags. If you buy just a few items, (unless they're the sort of things you would be embarrassed to carry out unwrapped--like double-fudge frosted brownies,etc.), don't even take a bag. Do get a receipt, though.

6. Support companies that make recycled paper products, which now include attractive greeting cards, books, magazines, containers, and other items. Although demand is increasing, it's still not enough to bring prices down. For recycling to pay off, consumers must request recycled products.

7. Save the Sunday comics to wrap children's presents. They also love to read the funnies later.

8. Re-use greeting cards, envelopes and wrapping paper. You probably wouldn't re-use an envelope for a job application, but you could use it to pay a bill.

9. Precycle when you buy products. Avoid those which are over-packaged. If you buy something that is excessively packaged, send the extra back to the manufacturer with a note encouraging less waste.

10. Give a tree as a gift. Don't buy your elderly Aunt Jenny another bottle of fancy perfume; give her a small tree, or a note promising to plant one in the spot of her choice. Hardwoods and evergreens work on bigger lots; potted trees are terrific on patios.

ADDICTED TO OIL?

1. Strive for at least one "car-less" day each week. Arrange to car pool to church, the football game, or a party. Allow time to walk to the post office, or take the bus. Give your car a rest (like in the old days, when people rested their hard-working horses.)

2. Keep your car well-tuned and change its oil often. It will run more efficiently and pollute the air less.

3. Buy a car that is as fuel-efficient as possible without giving up the safety features you want. Read reviews; talk to other car owners. For example, a car that gets 30 miles per gallon, if driven an average of 250 miles a week,will consume about 220 fewer gallons a year than a car thatgetsonly 20 miles to the gallon. This not only saves natural resources, it saves a considerable amount of money.

4. Request an energy audit of your home from your utility company. This can give you individualized suggestions for saving energy.

5. For small yards, use clippers, lawn mowers and other tools that are muscle-powered, not gasoline-powered. When possible, sweep a sidewalk rather than using a leaf blower. It's also good exercise.

6. Recycle your motor oil. Many service stations will handle your used oil. Buy recycled oil whenever possible. Most cars can use this cleaned, refined oil. If all drivers did this, we would decrease dependency on foreign oil. (New car owners--check your warranty first).

7. Break the habit of starting your car before everyone is ready to go, or letting it run while you wait for someone, adjust your mirror, or fasten your seatbelt. Most cars only need a few seconds to "warm up." The longer your car runs, the more pollution is spewed into the air.

8. Slow down and save fuel (and maybe even a life.) Driving too fast saves very little time. For example, if you are late for a meeting 30 miles away and you drive 70 miles an hour instead of 60, you will save only five minutes. A 120 mile trip at 70 miles an hour will take you one hour and 40 minutes; at 60 miles an hour it takes only 20 minutes more. Besides increasing your chances of an accident or a ticket, high speeds dramatically decrease fuel efficiency.

9. Try the renewable fuels such as ethanol. Support solar energy research. Write letters to car manufacturers and oil companies encouraging the development of more fuel-efficient vehicles.

10. Discover the joys of life sans windshields. Walk or bicycle through your neighborhood. You may be amazed at the fascinating people and places you whiz right by when in a car.

WATER, WATER, EVERYWHERE, BUT. . .

1. Brush your teeth, wash your face, and clean the tub without wasting gallons of water by running the water unnecessarily. Turn off the tap whenever you can.

2. Take short showers. Turn off the flow while you condition your hair. Bathe several small children together at the same time. Shower with your spouse.

3. A leaky faucet costs a lot. One drop per second wastes more than 200 gallons per month. Fix it.

4. Keep the water level high in your toilet tank with a simple water-filled bottle (or a special bag available at the utility company). Don't use a brick--it can break apart and clog your system. This displacement method will save water every time the toilet is flushed, which can add up to hundreds of gallons of water savings per month for a small family.

5. Keep the basin full of water in the kitchen or bathroom sink to wash your hands or rinse out rags while doing household chores. A refrigerated jug of water provides a cold drink without running water.

6. Don't insist on a spotless car. Washing your car uses a lot of water. When you do wash it, use a bucket and sponge; just hose it down for the final rinse.

7. If you notice water overflowing into the streets, gushing from a hydrant, or leaking from a broken public restroom tap, take the time to report it. Don't assume someone else will do it. Contact your local government office for a number to call.

8. Don't run your dishwasher or washing machine unless you have a full load. Investigate connecting your machines to an extra tank to catch the final rinse water. This "grey water" can be used for watering trees and bushes or washing cars.

9. Set up a big bucket or barrel in the backyard or patio to catch the rain so you can use it for watering plants or washing cars, bikes, or the dog.

10. Cut shower water use by almost 50% by installing a low-flow shower head (either aerated or nonaerated.) It conserves water and should pay for itself within a year. Estimates show that these gadgets can save the average household 3,000-4,000 gallons of water per person annually (the equivalent of a 15-year supply of drinking water for one person.) Check at your local hardware store or utility company (some provide them free of charge). You can also install, on faucets, low-flow faucet aerators. These are two extremely effective methods of home water conservation.

USE IT UP, WEAR IT OUT, RECYCLE IT OR DO WITHOUT! WHAT AND HOW?

1. Telephone books, newspapers and high-grade (mimeo, copy, computer, stationery) paper. Disgard any glossy inserts. Recycled newspaper is made into newsprint, insulation and cereal boxes, which saves trees.

2. Corrugated cardboard (corrugated boxes, egg and cereal cartons) Corrugated cardboard has two layers of heavy cardboard with a ribbed section between, and is commonly used for heavy-duty cartons. Flatten and bundle.

3. Aluminum (pop and beer cans, foil, food wrap, TV trays, pie plates) Rinse. Crushing isn't necessary. Aluminum from lawn furniture is also recyclable.

4. Glass (pop and beer bottles, mayonnaise jars, juice bottles, wine, liquor bottles, pickle, olive jars, ketchup bottles. Almost all glass except oven-proof) Rinse and separate bottles and jars by color. Recycled glass is used to manufacture new containers. Because lower temperatures are needed to make containers from recycled material, this saves energy.

5. Steel (tin) cans (food cans, non-aluminum cans)
Steel cans, often called tin cans, are usually food cans. They have side seams. To recycle, rinse, remove label, remove both ends and flatten. The market for tin cans is sometimes limited, so check with a local recycler.

6. Plastic (soft drink containers, milk containers, etc.)
At present, plastic recycling technology is new and the market is also somewhat limited. The following plastic items are recyclable at many recycling centers:

-milk & distilled water jugs
-oil & antifreeze containers
-bleach bottles
-certain household containers
-plastic shopping bags
-soft drink bottles

A nationally recognized voluntary material identification system for plastic has been developed. The Plastic Container Code System offers uniformity to bottle manufacturers and recyclers. Current codes, 1-7, are stamped on the bottom of the container. Find out which code numbers are recyclable or returnable in your community, and sort accordingly.

Look for recycling "reverse vending" machines that will give you cash for your bottles and cans. If there are no such machines in your town, try calling 1-703-591-1001, the Environmental Products Corporation, for information on these machines.

**Remember that it is important not to contaminate recyclables with color, food, or other foreign materials.

GOOD NEWS / BAD NEWS

BAD NEWS: Energy woes: fossil fuels are not renewable; nuclear power plants are risky, and hydropower destroys rivers and natural areas.

GOOD NEWS: Renewable solar energy and wind power sources are being slowly but steadily developed.

BAD NEWS: Canada, the source of much of the world's newsprint, cuts down 250,000 more acres of trees annually than it replants.

GOOD NEWS: A group of Los Angeles volunteers, the Tree People, planted a million trees before the 1984 Olympics. They continue to plant trees in the city.

BAD NEWS: Among those jumping on the trendy environmental bandwagon are shady dealers who deliberately mislead consumers as to the ecological wholesomeness of their products.

GOOD NEWS: At least two new non-profit companies, Green Cross of Oakland and Green Seal of Washington, D. C. will evaluate products for their actual impact on the environment. (*Atlantic Monthly*, October 1990)

BAD
NEWS: A car that gets 20 miles per gallon spews out about 52 tons of carbon dioxide in its lifetime.

GOOD
NEWS: A car that gets 45 miles per gallon emits only about 23 tons of CO_2 in its lifetime. A car that would get at least 60 mpg, as does a prototype developed by Volvo, would only add about 16 tons of carbon dioxide to the atmosphere, according to the Environmental Action Foundation.

BAD
NEWS: Due to off-shore drilling and leaking oil tankers, billions of gallons of clean sea water have been polluted. (Not to mention the sticky mess on shore and thousands of dead sea creatures).

GOOD
NEWS: The citizens of San Diego, California, when asked by their city council during the summer of 1990 to voluntarily cut back on water by 10%, actually decreased their water usage by 11% .

AND MORE
GOOD NEWS: This is the day that the Lord has made; let us rejoice and be glad.

If you hear about any environmental news (good or bad, local, national, international) send it to us at **Accord.** *If we use your contribution in a subsequent edition, we'll send you a free book or our canvas "Lord's Earth" bag (see page 111).*

Andrew

50

JUST FOR KIDS

"....for to such belongs the kingdom of heaven."
Matthew 19:13

No matter how old you are, you can help take care of the earth. Here are ten things you can do. How many more can you think of?

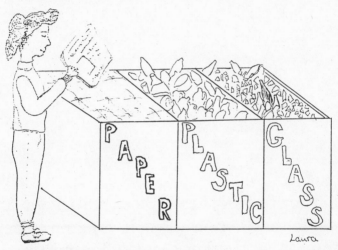

1. **Recycle** everything that can be recycled. Save soda pop cans, plastic containers, newspapers, used typing and notebook paper, and more. At school, at Sunday School and at home, help set up separate boxes so other kids can recycle, too. Ask your teacher or your parents to help you find a company to recycle these things for you. Some will even pay you for your help.

2. Turn off the light when you leave a room—unless, of course, your sister is still sitting in there! Turning out the lights when you don't need them saves electricity and conserves our natural resources.

3. Plant something. God created plants and people for each other. People breathe in oxygen and breathe out carbon dioxide. Plants use carbon dioxide to produce fresh, clean oxygen.

If you plant something from a seed or seedling and grow it inside in a pot or outside in the yard, you will be helping to clean the air and make the earth more beautiful. Ask your teachers at school and Sunday School if your class can plant something as a special project.

4. Turn off the water as you brush your teeth, wash dishes, or use the sink. And don't take long showers—more than five minutes is too long. When you leave the water running down the drain, you waste LOTS of good water that takes a lot of energy to clean and bring to your house. Just use what you need and turn the faucet OFF.

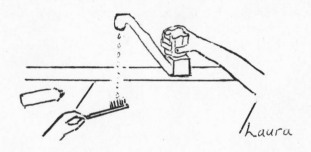

5. Be careful about what you use to eat and drink. Those white polystyrene "foam" cups and plates never go away. They take up a lot of room in our landfills, and big pieces can float out to sea.

If you go to a picnic or potluck, take your own plates, cups and silverware. You could carry them in a basket or bag. (And ask your parents to use real mugs for coffee and tea at work and at home.) This will help cut down on all the garbage that is littering God's green earth.

6. Stop and Think. Before you buy something or ask your parents to buy you something, look at it carefully. Do you really need it? Will it last a long time, or will it be used up, worn out or broken soon? Try not to add to the garbage problem, and don't buy more than you need. Don't buy food or drinks in containers than you can't recycle. Be an example to your friends.

7. Choose a special part of the earth and take care of it. Maybe it's the old creek in front of your house, or a litter-covered lot in your neighborhood, or your own backyard. Pick up trash, plant bushes, flowers or herbs, and help keep your special place clean and healthy.

8. Close the refrigerator and oven doors as quickly as you can after you open them. (Don't use your refrigerator for an air conditioner or your oven for a heater.) Get what you need and close the door. This will save electricity or gas, and help preserve the world's resources.

Andrew H.

9. Create a mini-wildlife refuge for birds, butterflies, ladybugs, squirrels, rabbits, deer and other "critters." Even if you live in the city, you can put plants and feeders on your windowsill or patio to attract some of these gentle creatures.

10. Pray for the healing of the earth, and that all who live here will respect what God has created.

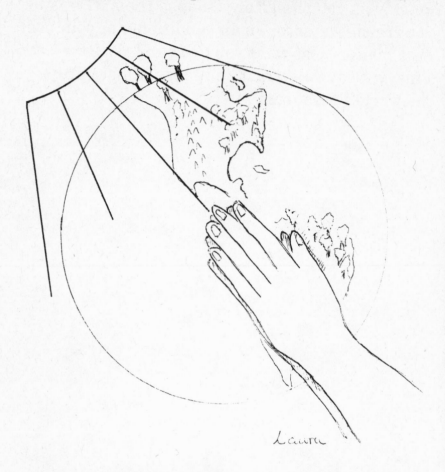

God bless you as you grow up helping to care for and protect the earth and all creation.

Part Three

The EARTH is the LORD'S
Handle with Care
©1990 Hesterman-Horst

*Reflections on
Creation and
Environmental
Responsibility*

ISSUES OF THE WALLET, ISSUES OF THE HEART

by Richard S. Greene

Four dollars--in the long run, big deal. But in the short run, spending four extra dollars appeared to be a senseless waste.

The more important issue, though, was protecting dolphins. My wife and I had been discussing for some time our aversion to purchasing tuna whose catch was destroying thousands of dolphins. One Saturday, with my three-year-old daughter along, I finally found cans of tuna with dolphin-safe labels. But it was premium white tuna, and each can was $1.04 more than the regular brand. Lynda needed four cans.

I genuinely agonized over whether to spend the extra $4.00. I wrestled with how deep my conviction was about helping, although in a small way, to preserve our environment by protecting wildlife. I explained quickly to my daughter the dilemma I was facing. I don't think she fully understood the issues, but she didn't hesitate to point to the blue dolphin symbol. I spent the extra money, and felt good about it when Lynda later applauded the decision.

When you consider the onslaught waged against the environment worldwide, my individual action that Saturday was miniscule. What impact did that make? I don't know. But before God, I knew I had to put teeth into my words. I do believe, however, that those tiny individual steps, when multiplied by similar actions taken by others and ones on an even broader scale, will be cumulative and can make a tremendous difference.

Two years ago, our Sunday school class studied various pressing social needs and how our Christian faith can effect change in those areas, both locally and nationally. The environment received equal play with abortion, poverty and pornography. Adding an element of urgency to our committee's argument was the Exxon oil spill disaster off Alaska.

I was proud of our class' reaction and how many instituted immediate changes. One couple started using cloth diapers instead of disposable ones. Most abandoned plastic milk containers, opting to buy cardboard cartons. Lynda and I now use paper instead of plastic to bag our groceries. Class members actively support our city's curbside recycling program of glass, aluminum cans and newspapers. When I collect grass clippings, I put them in a compost pile in the back corner of our yard, where Lynda grew several vegetables this summer. Riding the bus is a healthy alternative to driving my car every day.

Transforming our lifestyle is hard; breaking habits of convenience can be costly. One local newspaper recently reported that more than half of the garbage coming to the county's downtown Minneapolis incinerator can potentially be recycled instead of burned.

We can always do more. But why? What should be the motivation behind our behavior? We are obligated to the earth because God created it; it belongs to Him and we are its caretakers. Psalm 104 is a fascinating litany that describes God's magnificent creation. Verse 30 piques my curiousity: "When you send your Spirit, they are created, and you renew the face of the earth."

I don't completely comprehend what this Scripture entails, but somehow God's Holy Spirit is uniquely involved in the event of creation. He also participates in the restoration process. And I think, as believers under the control of the lordship of Jesus Christ, we can be in partnership with God in the renewal of His wonderful earth.

Therefore environmentalism and evangelicalism don't clash. We have a responsiblity to proclaim the Good News of Jesus Christ but to also live out His Word as agents of compassion and justice in a world at times darkened by tyranny, including the ravaging of the environment.

Denton Lotz, General Secretary for the Baptist World Alliance, wrote in the May 1990 BWA newsletter: In some churches there seems to be a conflict between those who emphasize saving souls and those who emphasize saving trees. This is a ridiculous conflict. We need saved souls who can live a meaningful life in God's beautiful world of nature, which itself is yearning to be free from pollution...Let's not confuse evangelism with ecology, but let's also show that true evangelists are also true ecologists working for that day when, as the Apostle Paul said, '...the creation itself will be set free from its bondage to decay and obtain the glorious liberty of the children of God.'" (Romans 8: 21)

That Biblical balance was absent at a recent program for ecumenical stewardship sponsored by a local interfaith ecology coalition. Evangelical Christians were overwhelmingly outnumbered by concerned people of other faiths and persuasions, including Zen Buddhists, Bahai's, Native American ritualists and Unitarians. They need my Jesus, but I need their spirit of environmental activism.

Each day I am reminded of my need to examine my attitude when I exit the door from work. A roadside billboard stabs at my conscience:

> *"The three biggest killers in America:*
> *cancer, heart disease and apathy."*

I pray I never fall prey to apathy. Saving $4.00 will never be the overriding issue. My mandate, and yours, is to conserve, preserve and enhance what God has given to us.

Richard S. Greene, a former newspaper journalist and communications director for the Navigators, is Associate Editor of Decision Magazine, the publication for the Billy Graham Evangelistic Association.

64

FOR LAND'S SAKE

by Bill Sy

My grandmother had a favorite expression, "For land's sake!"
It made us laugh whenever we heard it. Today those words make more
sense than ever. We are starting to recognize the irreplaceable value
of our land and other natural resources.

Years ago, 90% or more of the people tilled the soil. Now our
lifestyles have so changed that only three to four percent are commercial farmers. Most of us purchase milk, bread and meat from super-
market shelves. We have little awareness of the long journey these
foods take from the soil to the store.

It is easy to take for granted the earth's productivity. We are
reminded in Psalm 24:1 that the earth is not ours to abuse or misuse.
"The earth is the Lord's and the fulness thereof; the world and those
who dwell therein." It all belongs to God.

This is difficult for us to grasp. We tend to think the earth is ours,
or at least this certain parcel of ground is mine. We put down our
stakes and proudly claim our rights. Too many people can't see
beyond their limited possessions. They don't see the long-range
view. They don't see God's involvement in their life or possessions.

The Christian sees things differently. We know that God owns
it all. God has loaned it to us temporarily. We do the best we can
caring for what God has entrusted to us.

For the Christian, Jesus Christ is Lord. That means Christ is the
owner, the master of our possessions. He owns our material posses-

sions, our families, our lives. God allows us to use all these things for a time. But we are to be willing to let them go. If God sees that any of these things are hurting us or interfering with His plan for us, then we reliquish our ownership back to Him. All we have and are belongs to God. We are privileged to use these things in a way that pleases God.

After returning recently from a church camp, I noticed a sign: "Leave this place in better condition than when you came here." That would be a great motto for Christians. We can view our time here as pilgrims on a journey, determined to leave the earth in better shape than we found it.

We are only guests here on the Lord's earth. This isn't our home. We are invited to enjoy the facilities, and expected to keep up the property. If we begin to think we can control the earth without Him, we are no longer guests, we are trying to become lords. But there is only one Lord, Jesus Christ.

We are given a challenge to go into the world and make it a better place in the name of Jesus Christ. Our job as ambassadors for Christ is to make a positive difference in this world that Christ died to reconcile. (II Corinthians 5: 17-20)

God's creation waits with eager longing for the revealing face of God's children. (Romans 8:19) The whole world waits to see what a difference Christ makes in us, for we live with the dust of the earth in our shoes and the fire of heaven in our hearts.

Bill Sy is a speaker and a pastor at Vision of Glory Lutheran Church in Minneapolis.

OWLS, LUMBERJACKS, AND THE PLAN OF GOD

by Dean Ohlman

One major episode in the recent battle between the lumber industry and environmentalists was the placing of the northern spotted owl on the "Threatened Species" list by the U.S. Fish and Wildlife Service. This action requires the U.S. government to protects its habitat by reducing or even ending logging in the owl's range.

Although the decision was not a surprise, timber workers had hoped and prayed that it would be postponed. Now that it is official, it is expected that thousands of woodcutters will eventually lose their jobs and hundreds of mills will close. Environmentalists, by and large, are not sympathetic. They claim that the lumber industry has acted irresponsibly for decades by not replanting enough for future timber requirements, and by caring little about the protection of wildlife habitat. They also decry the sale of forest products to Japan causing more rapid depletion of our nation's forest reserves.

Forestry workers are understandably angry since they feel that the fate of human beings is more important than the fate of a subspecies that may become extinct in spite of this action. As they see it, eventually both logger and owl are destined for extinction. Among these lumber workers and their families, no doubt, are thousands of fellow believers who sincerely wish to know God's will regarding their futures.

Viewing this controversy from the perspective of Christian stewardship, unfortunately, does not make it any easier. The reason is that both sides of the argument have support from Scripture, and the amount of that support rests on the truth of the "facts" presented by the debaters.

Conservationists can present impressive data to show that both the federal government and the logging industry have been poor stewards of the forests, and that greed and materialism are fueling the demand for more wood. This is the true issue, not the fate of the owl. Environmentalists are using the bird to bring before the entire nation the question of values regarding the natural world. What is the value of man, what is the value of non-human animal species, what is the value of a tree (in some instances sold for less than what is paid for a Big Mac)?

Other questions for Christians arising from this debate are these: Is it good stewardship to fell thousands of trees for huge Sunday newspapers full of material that is never read in entirety by any subscriber—and will end up the following week in landfills that are nearly full? When millions of people around the world are homeless, is it Christian compassion for American believers to spend hundreds of thousands of dollars on lumber for ever larger homes? Is it wise use of God's marvelous creation to cut down thousand-year-old trees, destroy the habitat of ever more species, and disrupt fragile ecosystems in order to have neatly packaged individual meals to make our hectic lifestyles easier to maintain? If we are going to adjust our national economy to reflect better stewardship of our natural resources, isn't it inevitable that millions of workers nationwide will be temporarily unemployed as they make the adjustment from one industry to another?

On the other side of the debate are questions like these: Doesn't Scripture indicate that man is more important than animals? Isn't it biblically accurate to believe that God has given us these natural resources to use for man's benefit? Is it Christian compassion to put people through financial hardship and domestic turmoil to save an animal species that may already be doomed? Doesn't the cultural mandate in Genesis command us to fill the earth—and if that's true, isn't it natural for population growth to increase the demand for forest products?

Obviously all these questions are valid. And the way we answer them will likely have a profound effect upon the lives of all of us. In the process of answering them, however, the Christian must keep these biblical principles in mind:

1. *The earth is the Lord's, not man's. (Ps. 24:1-2; 1 Cor. 10:26)*

2. *Man has been given the task of stewardship regarding all of the earth's resources—both animals and forest products. (Gen. 1:26-30; Ps. 8:6-8)*

3. *What God created He called good and must not be despised or abused by man. (Gen. 1:25, 31)*

4. *Man and nature have been negatively affected by the Fall. One of the many negative effects has been disharmony between human beings, animals, and the land. (Gen. 3:17-19; Gen. 9:1-3, Ex. 23:29)*

5. *Through Christ's atoning death, the restoration of both man and nature was made possible. Though total restoration will come only at the physical return of Christ, partial restoration is possible here and now. Christians should be active in this restoration process. (Rom. 8:19-23)*

6. *Man, created in God's image, has the ability to reason and make rational choices based on moral values. Animals do not have these attributes and are at the mercy of man. (Isa. 1:18; Josh. 24:15; Deut. 30:19-20)*

7. *God, according to Scripture, gives man the right to use animals and plants, dead or alive, and utilize their products for his own benefit. (Gen. 9:1-3; Acts 10:10-15)*

8. *Scripture speaks often of the humane care and keeping of animals and does not support the senseless destruction of life. (Deut. 25:4; Prov. 12:10)*

9. *Scripture condemns waste and the careless use of land, and it speaks often of man's suffering loss as a result of greed and plunder. (Isa. 5:8; Ezek. 24:18-19; Hab. 2:17)*

10. *The earth will continue to show signs of wear and depletion until the time God brings about a new earth. (Isa. 51:6; 2 Pet. 3:5-13)*

Certainly there are other biblical concepts that have some application to this particular issue, but even these few indicate how difficult it is to resolve problems of this nature.

A further consideration here is the use of knowledge. Among the many things science and technology have done for us is to greatly increase the knowledge. And when knowledge increases, the importance of human responsibility increases. Many of our environmental crises have come about because of ignorance regarding the eventual consequences of various human activities. Once we know the results of our actions, however, we become responsible for our actions.

Because the whole cosmos suffers as a result of Adam's sin, we recognize that some human actions really come down to what we call "choosing the lesser of two evils." Nearly all human activities impact the natural world— many in a negative manner. Large-scale human industry in particular has the capacity to drastically alter the natural world. Just the simple growth of the human race and the resulting development required to provide food, clothing and shelter means the displacement or destruction of previously untouched nature. If not in the plan of God, this has long been a part of His sovereign will.

With the increase of knowledge, we now have a far greater understanding of man's impact on nature. Thus we now have a moral obligation to use that knowledge in a responsible manner. Some say that any human action which would result in the extinction of a species (an artificial, man-made distinction) is not acceptable. However, it is apparent that species extinction has always been a part of natural history—much of it not caused by man.

Is it possible that the disharmony brought about by the Fall of man is a major reason for this natural deterioration, and that until the restoration promised by the return of Christ, such negative consequences will be unavoidable? In other words, is the possible extinction of an animal species cause enough for human activity to be greatly altered? Perhaps this is merely one of the unavoidable facts of life in a fallen world.

Yet is it also possible that this knowledge is a gift of God intended to show us that our extravagant living and greed are raping nature and that to continue living in this manner will eventually bring about even greater human suffering and hardship? Perhaps it is time now for many industrial, agricultural, and commercial practices to be curtailed or ended before even greater harm is done to the ecosphere we share with all living things.

It is obvious that we Christians have a great challenge before us as we seek to be faithful to our God and to His Word regarding our stewardship of the earth. It is also obvious when we examine the controversy in the Pacific Northwest that many of these issues will not be easy to resolve. However, that must not deter us from taking on the task of applying biblical principles to all the interrelationships between man and the rest of the natural world.

Dean Ohlman is a writer, photographer and founding director of the Christian Nature Federation. This excerpt from the 1990 CNF Perspective used by permission.

GROWING UP AWARE

by Linda Ridley

I grew up in a home where the word "conservation" was never spoken, but always practiced. When we washed our hands, we half-filled the sink, soaped up and then rinsed under clear water. We learned that to wash under running water was wasteful, and soon it was second nature to close the sink stopper first.

My dad rigged up an extra tub to hold washing machine rinse water, so my mom could re-use the relatively clean water to rinse the next load. When the weather was extra dry, we saved that water still again, and hauled it in buckets to water the trees and bushes surrounding the house.

We rarely took long, leisurely showers. Water was precious, something to conserve.

We lived in a small rural town with no garbage pick-up, and always sorted the trash as we used it. Some went in the glass barrel, others in the metal barrel, and some in the burn barrel. Once or twice a year, Dad hauled these off to a local junkyard for recycling. Milk and pop came in glass bottles, which we washed and returned to the grocery store. Non-returnable glass jars were washed and re-used. Very little came in plastic containers.

We never questioned where to put trash when we weren't at

74

home. We held onto it until we found a trash can—period! To drop it on the ground was unthinkable. If we saw others litter,we were encouraged to pick it up ourselves.

My husband grew up in a home where cleanliness in the home and yard were also a priority. Trash was never allowed to accumulate and mar the environment.

Now as parents ourselves, my husband and I feel it is important to instill in our children a deep reverence for the earth which God created for us and gave us charge of. We try to practice as well as preach environmentalism to our children. We practice the obvious forms of environmentalism: the children help us to save and recycle clear glass, aluminum, newspapers. It is their job to smash pop cans and they share the profit from the recycling center. They know that we want to recycle plastic but can't find a local recycler. Instead, we try not to buy products in plastic.

We save all of our garbage, leaves, clippings and twigs and put them on a compost pile to put nutrients into our garden. The children take turns taking the garbage to the compost pile after every meal.

Our children, too, have learned to respect the land. They were stunned one day when someone in the car in front of us threw a trash-filled fast-food bag out the window. After asking us what had come out of the car window, they asked why the people threw it out. All three were unable to fathom someone doing this rather than saving it for a trash can.

The heritage of saving water is being passed on to our children. We save our bath water and laundry rinse water to water our flowers, trees and gardens in the summer. We use organic soaps and cleaners. I hang my clothes on the line whenever I can to give them a sweet outdoor fresh scent rather than using artificially perfumed products.

I believe that the earth is being despoiled because of industrialism and greed. Therefore, along with practicing environmental care in our lives, I preach and try to practice self-sufficiency as much as possible. If we depend on others to produce everything for us, then we can't really control how those products are made, or what the production of these products does to the environment.

Although we live in a small town, we raise almost all of our own food. We made part of our back yard into vegetable and herb gardens in which we use only rotation and other organic controls. We also have raspberries, strawberries and some fruit trees. We never use chemicals, even on these. Picking off bad fruit as we find it, planting herbs with scents that repel insects, and realizing that we don't need more than we can eat in one year are ways we control pests and get a harvest adequate for ourselves.

We buy chickens from a farmer who raises them in a clean, humane environment and uses untreated feed. We try to buy beef in the same manner. My husband eats red meat, but the children and I prefer whole grains and legumes with lots of fresh vegetables. For what we don't raise ourselves, we use mostly organic foods purchased at a natural food store.

Not long ago, my daughter and her friend were discussing the merits of peanut butter. My little girl felt hers was real, because it was freshly made from whole peanuts with nothing added. Her friend said hers was the real stuff, because it was a name brand (made with sugar, hydrogenated oils, salts and preservatives).

When the children ask why we don't have a new van like some of their friends do, I tell them we will never buy a brand new vehicle if I have my choice. I feel that to constantly buy new things encourages over-production. If we buy a used car, keep it well-tuned and in good shape, then we are not causing as many cars to be produced.

I would like to altogether eliminate the need for gasoline-powered cars, for garden tools that use gasoline, and for gas heat and power. I hope that we are raising children who will care enough to support research in the effective, individual use of solar energy.

Recently, a friend's professor showed her class a map of all the buried nuclear and toxic wastes. He asked the students to suggest solutions. When my friend suggested that production of such wastes be stopped, he said that was a totally unrealistic idea, as it would interfere too much with our comfort, with industry and with the structure of society.

I want my children to see reality through God's eyes and not through men's. Reality is not the wasteful industrial society of today, a society that can't seem to understand that producing toxic wastes of any kind is unrealistic. It destroys what is real in the world that God so lovingly, artistically created for us.

Reality is this: that God made the world with certain controls and limitations. If we don't honor these, we suffer. I hope we are raising children—God's children—who will not only practice environmental care in their own lives, but also help fight the waste and greed that can destroy this world.

HOW TO RAISE AN ENVIRONMENTALIST

1. Be one. Never preach what you don't practice. Actions always speak louder than words.

2. Ask for God's guidance to show you how you are damaging His creation, and how to better care for it. (In our lives, He has clearly shown us the need for eating organic foods and the dangers of chemicals of all kinds, so we now never buy chemical products that will be harmful to us or to the earth.)

3. Make it meaningful to the children. Let them smash the cans, bundle the paper, go along to the recycling center and share in the profits.

4. Discuss landfills with your children. Go to one on a family field trip.

5. Pray with your children for God to protect and restore the earth until the day of His return.

Linda Ridley, a former high school home economics teacher, is now a homemaker and mother of three children. She teaches them at home, in association with the Northwestern Ohio Christian Homeschooling Organization.

CORNFODDER, EXHAUST, AND HAZARDS

by Vern Hesterman

Most Christians are aware of our Lord's admonition in Mark and Luke to be good stewards. Do we practice good stewardship when we permit our natural resources to be used so voraciously that future generations—or even our own—may experience real shortages?

We expect the luxury of comfortable private auto transportation from home to portal, resulting in countless vehicles carrying one or two passengers. Convoys of monstrous semi-trucks travel the same routes, each with separate engines. Mass transit would be more efficient, albeit not always as convenient.

We demand more and more gasoline-powered entertainment in our leisure time. Auto-racing, boating, and all-terrain vehicle driving are just a few examples.

We devour our precious oil with war maneuvers and training exercises so that we will be prepared to protect our vital interests (namely, our source of oil).

We tear out woodlots and forests, and we drain our wetlands to have more land for farming. Then, overproduction causes prices to fall too low.

Modern farmers have been encouraged to boost production by the use of chemicals such as herbicides, pesticides, and commercial fertilizers. True, these practices boost production, but more and more evidence is mounting that our health is adversely affected by them.

How long can our soil remain rich and fertile? Is it being robbed of necessary nutrients by intensive farming practices and artificial additives? Perhaps some incurable illnesses such as cancer are caused because the soil is deficient in certain elements humans need. Soil in the Great Lakes region, for instance, lacks iodine. Before this was discovered and iodine added to the diets, people suffered from goiters.

Look at a cornstalk. We plant a tiny seed, and a miracle happens. A huge stalk with an ear or two comes out of the ground. We harvest it, leaving the ground bare. Surely some vital elements are taken from the soil to produce so much from one little seed.

Unlike in the past, today when hay and straw is harvested, often nothing is returned to the land. Commercial fertilizer is usually applied, but no one knows if it really replenishes all the nutrients taken from the soil.

When I was a boy, most people practiced early conservation methods—unknowingly, perhaps, but effectively. Vehicles were only used for necessary transportation. Prepackaging was unheard of, produce was canned or preserved, and the containers were recyled in the home. Farmers returned all crops back to the soil, by plowing under the residue or the manure produced by the livestock which ate the crop. One-fourth of every farm was left idle or in pasture every year, because all farmers practiced crop rotation.

I grew up on a farm, and can still recall the concern of the local farmers when a neighbor replaced his horses with a tractor and began raising soybeans as a cash crop. "Why, he'll ruin the soil!" they said, shaking their heads. In their love of the land was concern for the well-being of future generations.

Farming in pre-tractor days was much more labor-intensive than today, and every member of the family was expected to help, including the women and children. Farm life was, however, by no means dull. Neighbors gathered frequently to visit and often enthusiastically participated in home-made ice cream eating contests.

At harvest time, neighbors also helped each other with grain threshing rings. A mark of manhood was being able to carry a sack of grain from the threshing machine to the grain bins, sometimes even up a flight of stairs. While the adults worked in the fields or prepared the meals, the young children played all day long. After the work was done everyone—men, women and children—feasted on sumptuous, delicious homemade food.

Farm life in those days was not all idyllic, though. People got kicked by horses or cows, chased or bitten by

hogs, rams, roosters and ganders. Runaway teams of horses were also a frequent hazard, as I found out firsthand when I was about 16.

While mowing hay with a horse and mule team, I somehow disturbed a bumblebee's nest. The bees swarmed all over the team, which suddenly took off on a wild gallop, throwing me off. The bumblebees immediately attacked me and I took off in the opposite direction, flailing away at them with my straw hat. The results of this episode were five broken fence posts, a broken hay mower, a severely stung and sick driver and an unmowed field of hay.

A few years earlier, I had had another close call as I was helping put up hay. We used a team of horses, with ropes and pulleys, to pull a sling full of hay from a loaded wagon up to the ceiling of the barn and over into the hay mow. My job was to pull down on the end of the rope at

the opposite side of the barn to return the empty slings.

Sometime during the day, I got a bright idea. I thought that if I held on to my end of the rope as the horses pulled the sling up, I would get a free ride up to the top of the barn.

I figured that after the hay was deposited in the mow, my weight would bring the empty sling back as I rode down again.

However, as the horses began pulling their rope and I headed towards the barn ceiling, I realized the flaw in my plan—I had misjudged how much rope would be pulled up, and I was ascending too fast. From my vantage point, it didn't look like the horses would stop before I reached the pulley high above. I loosened my grip to slide back down, and ended up with severe rope burns on my hands and a sheepish look on my face. That was better, though, than being pulled right on through that pulley up at the highest point inside the barn.

There's no question that progress has made farming easier, more efficient and in some ways, less dangerous than in the days of runaway horses and high-swinging hay slings. However, our grandparents' old-fashioned lifestyles may have merit after all, even in these modern times. Their careful use of natural resources provides an example of good stewardship for Christians today. Someday, perhaps soon, progress may come to mean re-examining and returning to some of those old ways.

Vern Hesterman, a member of St. Peter's Evangelical Lutheran Church, has been a high school teacher, coach and guidance counselor in Northwest Ohio's Ridgeville and Four-County schools. Although officially retired, he still teaches part-time and does a bit of fishing and farming.

LIVING SABBATICALLY

by Gerard Reed

Since God rested on the seventh day of creation, entering into an eternal sabbath of delight at His work, He told His people to remember the Sabbath, to make it holy.

To live sabbatically means awakening to an acute awareness of God-in-Creation. The Creation account reveals that God rested on the seventh day. He wasn't tired. He didn't need to recover His strength. He rested in order to enjoy what He'd made. Having called into being creatures of great worth, God determined to reflect upon, to interact with, to appreciate His work. God freely created, which is to say "out of love."

Rightly read, the Old Testament calls for three different kinds of Sabbath: one day out of seven, one year out of seven, and a culminating jubilee year to consummate a 50-year cycle. This plan provided for rest and restoration for humans and for the land.

The reality of the sabbath is this: while work is necessary, it is not the one thing necessary. We need to stop the compulsive busyness which characterizes our normal routines. We need to slow our furious quest for money and man-sions. We need to just stop and be God's children.

Living sabbatically, resting from labor, resting in the Lord's land, just letting creation be, pursuing simple activities which add nothing to our bank accounts—all illustrate ecological wisdom and surrender to God's will.

Though lots of folks rest once a week in our society, the second sabbatical commanded in Scripture is almost nowhere practiced. God commanded His people to rest every seventh year, and to allow creation itself to rest as well. Were this universally practiced, we'd have had far less bad news on Earth Day, 1990. Earth's soil is a marvelous organic mix of living creatures. Since farming takes nutrients from the soil, it need periodic rest and restoration. Good farming rests the soil. Good cultures encourage and support good agriculture.

We can't very easily reinstate the ancient society which received the sabbatical commands. We can, however, apply to our lives today some relevant principles:

1. Recognize God's Lordship/Ownership

When we once recognize that everything is really God's, we're less compulsive about work and ownership. Pausing regularly to celebrate the Lord's Day, in fact, greeting every day as the Lord's Day, is a way of worshipping.

2. Respect and revere God's handiwork.

The older I get, the more I agree with Malcom Muggeridge, who discovered in his advanced years, that few pleasures exceed simply watching each day's sunrise...each day's sunset. Certainly it's a great joy to see sunrises and sunsets—if they happened twice a year we'd be overwhelmed by their beauty. Since they're routine, we fail to value them. We need—most of us at least—to learn the simple joy of just enjoying and respecting the world's beauty.

3. *Reject consumerism (covetousness).*

Though not as obviously destructive as alcoholism, America's commitment to getting and spending—a mix of workaholism and consumerism—may be more deeply injurious to the spirit. We live in a consumer society. To consume means to use up, to devour; earlier generations called tuberculosis "consumption" for it literally sucked life out of a person. And our record is clear: we're devouring the earth. Consumers make waste, and we're wasting our only home.

Were we to live sabbatically, we'd scoff at advertisements' lies, for we know that "man does not live by bread alone, but by every word which comes from the mouth of the Lord." Regularly, routinely, daily, we'd stop the work-harder-spend-more binge of consumerism.

4. *Redistribute wealth.*

The Bible clearly calls for justice—the proper distribution of the earth's resources. Yet it nowhere insists that everyone should have exactly the same amount. Sabbatical principles indicate how we can rightly distribute earth's bounty.

For one thing, if we don't work all the time, there's work for others to do so they can make their own livings. When we give away our surplus (the "gleanings" left on the edges of the fields), we help the needy. When we give tithes and offerings to the Church, we help money circulate in compassionate ways. When we support responsible environmental groups, we redistribute our wealth in healing, environmentally-wise ways. Sabbaatical living means knowing when enough is enough, and then sharing earth's dividends with others.

5. *Relax and be what we are.*

"Man does not live by bread alone," Jesus said. Work must be kept in its rightful place; it should be integrated

86

with, merely a part of, our being the persons we're called to be.

6. *Restore our Lost Perfection.*

Adam and Eve, before their fall from the Garden of Eden, lived a meaningful life of leisure. They didn't survive by the sweat of their brows—they simply accepted the riches of paradise. So, in a related sense, the Sabbath gives us a taste of Paradise—the quiet, at-ease condition for which God made us.

I am a Wesleyan, and we believe in Christian "perfection," becoming the men and women God designed us to be through God's gracious delivery from sin's penalty and bondage. We believe that we can cooperate with God in reconsituting and restoring the world He originally designed. And this we do, primarily, by learning to live sabbatically, following the pattern of Paradise.

Dr. Paul Brand, a great Christian who spent many years as a missionary doctor in India, fears the very wellspring of life may be perishing. While he had been tending needy lepers, the land had been despoiled. He would give up medicine, he said recently, if he could have some influence on environmental policies. "The world will die from lack of soil and pure water long before it will die from lack of antibiotics or surgical skill and knowledge," he warns.

Perhaps, just perhaps, if millions of other believers would catch a vision of what could be done to heal the earth as well as human bodies, the environmental crisis could be eased and ultimately ended.

*Gerard Reed is a professor and college chaplain at Point Loma Nazarene College in San Diego. This excerpt is from his manuscript **Holy His Land: Caring for Creation,** Copyright 1990. Used by permission.*

AS WE WAIT

by Gloria John Splittgerber

*For the creation waits with eager longing for
the revealing of the sons of God.* Romans 8:19

The 1989 oil spill in Prince William Sound, Alaska, was another sad example of God's created earth suffering at the hands of God's people. God gave Adam and Eve and their descendants responsibility to care for the earth. Throughout history, the management has been disastrous, for just as sin damaged our relationship with our Creator, so it damaged our relationship with the creation.

Someday, this negative situation will be reversed. We will be free of the bondage of sin. We will have sinless physical bodies to go along with our redeemed spirits that have been washed clean by the blood of Jesus. Likewise the world will be free of physical decay. The environment will again enjoy the perfect balance that was destroyed in the Garden of Eden. Until then, we—and nature—wait with eager expectations.

*Gloria John Splittgerber is a writer and member of St. John's Lutheran Church in Oshkosh, Wisconsin. (From **Christ In Our Home,**July 28, 1990.) Copyright 1990 Augsburg Fortress. Used by permission.*

ON TREES

by Vicki Hesterman

I discovered early that a sturdy tree branch high above my usual world was the perfect place to daydream. And if I didn't feel like climbing, I could relax with a book and an apple in the shaded sanctuary of our big old sycamore. That giant of a tree had known dozens of rough embraces from the neighborhood children who safely reached its home-free trunk during twilight games of Hide and Seek.

When I was growing up in northwestern Ohio, you couldn't walk a country mile without passing thick groves of trees and natural woodlots, which was just fine with me. Those woods were lovely, dark and deep—and full of adventures.

As long as I live, I will not forget the clear, brisk day when I returned home early from school and saw to my horror that most of our trees were gone. I ran back to the once tree-lined "crick" a quarter-mile behind our house, and just wept. All were dead—the big oaks, the magnificent elms, the gnarled old wild cherry, apple and pear trees. There they lay, their branches stretching up towards the sky.

My family was as stunned as I was. These trees were beloved old friends. We later learned that a work crew had passed through the area that morning, cleaning the county drainage waterways that flowed through private land, and cutting down any troublesome trees. It turned out to be a bureaucratic mistake, which was little consolation. Our trees were gone.

That was 25 years ago. Today, trees once again grow along that little country creek. Some sprang up wild from the seeds of the original trees; others we carefully planted with hope.

To travel this country is to pass by thousands of acres of woods and forests—trees of all kinds. The lush hardwoods of Michigan thrive, from the shores near Sleeping Bear Dunes to the isolated northern grandeur of Tahquemmonen Falls. In Wyoming's Tetons, tall pines line Jenny Lake and shelter the moose and deer that live in the shadows of the mountains.

Maples grow crimson in the Minnesota autumn and attract singing birds all year long. In a photograph now framed on my wall, an orange-breasted robin huddles on a snow-covered branch, resting just outside my bedroom window one frigid Minnesota morning. Up north, in the unspoiled wilderness of the Boundary Waters, velvety green islands are perfect places to land a canoe, lean back against a rugged pine, and marvel at the serenity and the smell of the air.

A bicycle ride through rural Georgia in the springtime can be an unforgettable visual experience, filled with delicate pink and white dogwood blossoms, magnificent creamy magnolia trees in full flower, and rich purple redbuds. Sometimes the kudzu vines grow over entire trees, creating eerie and unearthly shapes.

And in California, the trees—from the enormous red-woods and sequoias of the north to the no-nonsense palms and torrey pines of the south—help filter the air and preserve some natural beauty in a state of ever-growing freeways, congestion and air pollution alerts. Incredibly, trees thrive on our waste, carbon dioxide, and produce fresh, cool, clean air. We need trees; they need us.

Although I have moved to a delightful city bounded by the Pacific Ocean, San Diego Harbor and several bays, I live a bit inland on a canyon. As much as I love the sea, I love trees more.

Every morning, when I open my curtains and look out over the vast expanse of greenery that shelters wildlife—hawks and coyotes and rabbits—here in the middle of a big city, I feel refreshed and renewed. My reverent response to the simple beauty of the trees is wordless praise to the Lord of all creation. Their very existence exemplifies the creative, practical nature of our God.

When I see a tree, I see a wondrously intricate organism that, while alive, provides beauty, clean air, and a home for wild creatures. I know that later its body and branches may become paper for books and wood for shelter. Some say they need a miracle to really believe that God exists. When I see a tree, I have seen **a miracle**.

Vicki Hesterman is a writer, photographer and college professor in San Diego, California, with roots in Ohio.

ARE WE RESPONSIBLE
FOR THE EARTH?

by John Emil Halver

Professor of fish nutrition in the College of Ocean and Fishery Sciences at the University of Washington in Seattle, John Halver, Ph. D., was elected to the National Academy of Sciences in 1978. He has been trying for 40 years to "help people around the world improve their economy and their food availability and protein supplies so that they can grow and develop normally." Dr. Halver, a Methodist, feels that some Christians use the excuse that Christ is coming again, so they don't need to be concerned about using up the earth's resources. He says that "whether He returns now or 1,000 years from now, we had better have a plan of responsible stewardship."

The environment is the whole system that supports an ecosystem. Fish are one part of it. Water is essential because it's the major solvent for all of our life processes. As the world's population increases and as technology develops, we have more and more effluent materials entering our water systems. These vary from highly eutrophied ponds and oxidation sewage systems to pristine mountain lakes that are being affected by acid rains.

Many of these water bodies have the capability to recover. Lake Washington in the Seattle area was almost lost through eutrophication and effluent contamination. It required serious efforts to change the loading of its water environment. But Lake Washington has recovered and is now productive.

What bothers me is the stewardship of our resources. I am not a person who feels that we can live in a no-risk world. We have logical risks that we accept all the time. But we are having an impact on our natural resources. When we dump wastes into our rivers and they spill into the sea, the water quality changes. The Rhine River in Europe now is not the Rhine during the days of Charlemagne when the river had salmon runs. This change came about because of the needs of an expanding industrial world.

Parts of our environment are decaying faster than they can be regenerated. Forests in the Middle East and in Africa are being chopped down for fuel, but they are not being replaced fast enough. But they cannot be replaced without an adequate source to be used instead of the forests. Tension will also exist between meeting our industrial needs and preserving our environment.

To subdue [as in God's command in Genesis 1:28 to "subdue the earth"] does not mean to abuse. I think the earth's natural resources are here for our wise and judicious use, not for our irrational or selfish use. A balance is needed between the use of fertilizers in agriculture and the increase of phosphates and nitrates and other elements needed for agricultural production.

Many of us do not want to sit down and face the issues in life and the questions in the Bible. We prefer to defer them or to rationalize our complacency. These questions are personal; they are to be settled between us and God. They deal with whether or not we are good stewards of all the talents and resources that God has given to us as a nation and as individuals. When we examine these questions, most of us, including me, have woefully inadequate answers.

We have to study and look behind the sensational or dogmatic statements made by zealots of one program or another. Ask sincere questions, including "How big or severe is the problem?" "Where do I fit in?" and "What can be done?" Couple your questions with concern. Commit yourself, make a pledge: "I will do this and change my way of life a little bit here." Then tell your friends.

Plant a tree. Maintain a garden. Keep your lawn in shape with a minimal use of chemicals.

Don't be careless. For example, our streets and waters are littered with plastic wraps, jugs and containers. Start at home. Plastic can be recycled and reused. Also collect and recycle all your glass containers, aluminum cans and newspapers. It takes a little effort, but if everybody did this, we would see a major change.

To help combat the attack on our ecosystem, my wife and I try to be frugal and to keep our living standards from being exorbitant. We live in Seattle, but also have a 30-acre farm in the Columbia River Gorge area where 10 acres are kept as a woodlot for deer, turkeys and grouse. It is an environment that ensures a quality of natural life. We seed our fields with subterranean clover to maintain the natural nitrogen fixation so that we don't have to use so much inorganic fertilizer. We have some 40 fruit trees and use a lime-sulphur base for winter spray; we do minimal spraying to cut down on insect infestation.

My wife and I try to be reasonable stewards of our property, our lives and our time. We are involved in our church, and we try to be good neighbors and take part in community events.

I believe that God is the author of truth and logic and that science is the precision of this truth. I see no conflict between science and theology, and I believe that science and truth are on a convergent path.

I envision exciting solutions for many things. I am confident that we will have a breakthrough in using solar energy and in generating fusion energy. We rely too much on oil and gas. They are fine for certain applications, but we are not using them effectively. I also think that we will see improvements in the use of fision energy, which is one of the safest power supplies we have.

Christians can help shape environmental legislation. I think we can influence government officials; one person can make a difference if he or she draws enough attention to a problem.

We need to stop and think how wonderfully fortunate we are. I believe that the world was created by God and that He has a concern for it. When evil occurred, God came to change it through Jesus Christ. Those who believe in Christ claim him as their personal Savior. Since I believe that, I have hope.

We do not understand many things about the world, but as we unravel them, we can use this knowledge in a positive manner. If we are thankful for our existence and the environment in which we live, we will be good stewards of the resources. We don't know how long we will have to use them.

*Dr. Halver's article is from an interview with Richard Greene, **Decision Magazine**, November, 1989. Copyright 1989 Billy Graham Evangelistic Association. Used by permission.)*

Part Four

The EARTH is the LORD'S
Handle with Care
©1990 Nesterman-Hurst

Who
Can We Call?
What
Should We Read?
Where
Do We Write?

Therefore do not lose heart.
Though outwardly we are wasting away,
yet inwardly we are being renewed
day by day.

2 Corinthians 4: 16

*The following organizations and institutes are
dedicated to celebrating and healing the Lord's earth:*

CHRISTIAN NATURE FEDERATION

"Celebrating the Wonder of God's Creation," is the motto of a new nature association with a distinctive Christian foundation, CNF already has 500 members across the country. Expeditions, a stock photo service, environmental awareness activities, conservation evangelism, seminars and publications are in the planning.

Former astronaut **Jim Irwin** enthusiastically supports CNF, as can be seen in his statement beginning on page 11 and continued here:

"...When I learned about the Christian Nature Federation and its goal to renew the Christian's respect and awe for God's creative handiwork, I was thrilled. Actually, CNF is the kind of organization that should have begun decades ago—when we first came to realize how unique and fragile the earth truly is. It is my hope and prayer that thousands of Christians will become a part of the Christian Nature Federation so that the world may know not only of the church's concern for the earth, but also of our concern for the souls of men."

From the CNF credo, the *Earthkeeper's Understanding*:

"I believe that a Personal, Caring God created the Heavens and the Earth, and that He created Mankind in His own Image. I understand the Human Beings are unique in all of Creation: Endowed alone with the ability to Reason and to make Moral Choices, Mankind has a Superior Position over the rest of Creation which involved a God-given Authority and Responsibility to care for it as a good Steward..."

Contact: Dean Ohlman, Christian Nature Federation, P.O. Box 33000, Fullerton, California 92633 (714) 447-9673

AU SABLE INSTITUTE OF
ENVIRONMENTAL STUDIES

Michigan's Au Sable Institute of Environmental Studies, an educational institution affiliated with the Christian College Coalition, sponsors workshops, forums, classes and publications dedicated to increasing the interest in the environment and environmental stewardship. Students from all over the country attend summer sessions for credit. Director Cal De Witt, who is also professor of Environmental Studies at the University of Wisconsin, says, "It appears that the Christian world is turning a corner—there appears to be a 'paradigm shift' that is putting the environment and creation's integrity right at its center. And included in this shift are those who profess to follow the 'one by Whom everything was made and through Whom all things hold together.'"

Contact: Au Sable Institute of Environmental Studies, 7526 Sunset Trail N. E., Mancelona, Michigan, 49659

ELCA ENVIRONMENTAL TASK FORCE

This group of concerned Christians is developing a theologically-based stimulus for churchwide education on environmental responsibility. The Commission for Church in Society, of which it is part, works to increase awareness of environmental responsibility, world hunger, and related issues through speakers, seminars, books, pamphlets and videotapes, available through the main office.

Contact: Commission for Church in Society, Evangelical Lutheran Church in America, 8765 W. Higgins Road, Chicago, IL 60631 1-800-638-3522

FLORESTA

Poverty, deforestation and global warming are advancing hand-in-hand, according to FLORESTA, a San-Diego based organization dedicated to helping subsistence farmers in developing countries learn healthier and more efficient farming habits that will not destroy the world's virgin forests. The group, founded by Thomas Woodard, also provides loans, training, tree nurseries, and other projects dedicated to fostering self-sufficiency in developing countries. "Floresta has found a way to stop the devastating environmental degradation caused by deforestation while providing communities with alternative income-generating opportunities," says World Vision executive director Paul Thompson about the organization.

Contact: Ken Sauder, Executive Director, Floresta, 1015 Chestnut Avenue Suite F-2, Carlsbad, CA 92008

Editor's note: This is not intended to be an exhaustive list of such groups; let us know if you would like to be considered for inclusion in a subsequent edition.

MAGAZINES and PAMPHLETS
ON RELATED ISSUES (CHRISTIAN AND SECULAR)

The Amicus Journal
122 East 42nd Street Rm 4500
Natural Resources
 Defense Council
New York, NY 10168

Au Sable Institute Publications
7526 Sunset Trail NE
Mancelona, MI 49659

Christian Nature Federation
Publications
P.O. Box 33000
Fullerton, CA 92633

Does God Exist?
Donmoyer Ave. Church of Christ
718 East Donmoyer Ave.
South Bend, IN 46614

Earthwatch
680 Mount Auburn Street
 P.O. Box 403
Watertown, Mass. 02272

The Egg: Journal of Eco-Justice
Anabel Taylor Hall
Cornell University
Ithica, NY 14853

Environment
4000 Albemarle St.
Washington, D.C. 20016

Environmental Action
1525 New Hampshire Ave.
NW Washington, D.C. 20036

Garbage
 435 Ninth St.
 Old House Journal Corp.
 Brooklyn, NY 11215

Harrowsmith-on Country Living
The Creamery
 Charlotte, VT 05445

International Wildlife.
1412 16th St. NW
National Wildlife Fed.eration
Washington, DC 20036

National Parks.
 1015 31st Street
 Washington 20007

Nature Conservancy Magazine
1815 North Lynn Street
Arlighton, VA 22209

Natural History Magazine
79th and Central Park W
New York, NY 10024

Oceans
 2001 W. Main Street
 Stamford, CT. 06902

Oceanus
Woods Hole Oceanographic Inst.
 Woods Hole, MA 02543

Sea Frontiers
 3979 Rickenbacker Causeway
 Virginia Key   Miami, FL 33149

FOR MORE INFORMATION
(A selection of secular and Christian sources)

**Au Sable Institute
of Environmental Studies**
7526 Sunset Trail N.E.
Mancelona, MI 49659

Christian Nature Federation
P.O. Box 33000
Fullerton, CA 92633

**Committee on
Social Witness Policy**
Presbyterian Church (USA)
100 Witherspoon Building
Louisville, KY 40202

Degradable Plastics Council
1000 Executive Parkway
St. Louis, MO 63141

**Environmental
Task Force**
Commission--Church in Society
Evangelical Lutheran
Church of America
8765 W. Higgens Road
Chicago, IL 60631

**Environmental Hazards
Management Institute**
P.O. Box 932
10 Newmarket Road
Durham, NH 03824

**Environmental
Protection Agency**
401 M Street SW
Washington, D.C. 20001
(202) 554-1080

**Land/Natural Resources
Division
Department of Justice**
10th and Constitution Ave.
Washington, D.C. 20002

Floresta U.S.A., Inc.
1015 Chestnut Avenue Suite F2
Carlsbad, CA 92008

**General Board of
Church and Society**
The United Methodist Church
100 Maryland Avenue NE
Washington, DC 20002

**Household Hazardous
Waste Project**
901 South National Avenue
Box 108
Springfield MO 65804

**Humane Farming
Association**
1550 California Street Suite 6
San Francisco, CA 94109

**The North American
Conference on
Christianity and Ecology**
P.O. Box 14305
San Francisco, CA 94114

Recycle America
Waste Management Inc.
3003 Butterfield Road
Oak Brook, IL 60521

FOR FURTHER READING

Austin, Richard Cartwright. *Baptized into Wilderness: A Christian Perspective on John Muir.* Atlanta: John Knox Press, c. 1987.

_____. *The Beauty of the Lord: Awakening the Senses..* Atlanta: John Knox Press, 1988.

_____. *Hope for the Land: Nature and the Bible.* Atlanta: John Knox Press, 1988.

Berry, Wendell. *The Gift of Good Land.* San Francisco: North Point Press, 1981

Bowman, Douglas C. *Beyond the Modern Mind: The Spiritual and Ethical Challenge of the Environmental Crisis.* New York: The Pilgrim Press, c. 1990.

Brown, Lester, et. al. *State of the World.* Washington, D.C.: Worldwatch Institute, 1989

Brand, Paul and Philip Yancey. *Fearfully and Wonderfully Made.* Grand Rapids: Zondervan Publishing House, 1980

_____. *In His Image.* Grand Rapids: Zondervan, 1984.

Caplan, Ruth. *Our Earth, Ourselves.* Bantam Books, 1990.

Carson, Rachel. *Silent Spring.* Boston: Houghton Mifflin Company, 1962.

Center for Science in Public Interest. *99 Ways to a Simple Lifestyle.* Anchor Press/Doubleday, 1977.

Crisis in Eden: A Religious Study of Man and Environment. Abingdon, Nashville, TN, 1970.

The EarthWorks Group. *50 Simple Things You Can Do to Save the Earth.* Berkely: Earthworks Press, 1989.

Dillard, Annie. *Pilgrim at Tinker Creek: A Mystical Excursion into the Natural World,* New York: Bantam Books, 1975.

Ehrenfeld, David. *The Arrogance of Humanism.* New York: Oxford University, 1978.

Elkington, John, Julia Hailes and Joel Makowe. *The Green Consumer: You Can Buy Products that Don"t Cost the Earth.* Viking Penguin, 1990.

Fox, Matthew. *Original Blessing: A Primer in Creation Spirituality.* Santa Fe: Bear & Co., 1983.

Global 2000 Report to the President,. Report prepared by the Council on Environmental Quality and the Department of Energy, 1982.

Granberg-Michaelson, Wesley. *Ecology and Life: Accepting Our Environmental Responsibility.* Waco: Word Books, 1988.

_____, ed. *Tending the Garden: Essays on the Gospel and the Earth.* Grand Rapids: Wm.B. Eerdmans, 1987.

Hall, Douglas John. *The Steward.* Grand Rapids: Eerdmans/Friendship Press, 1990.

Krueger, Frederick, Ed. *Christian Ecology: Building an Environmental Ethics for the 21st Century.* San Francisco: North Amrican Conference of Christianity and Ecology, Inc., 1988.

Joranson, Philip, and Butigan, Ken, eds. *Cry of the Environment: Rebuilding the Christian Creation Tradition. Santa Fe: Bear and Co., 1984.*

Lamb, Marjorie. *Two Minutes a Day for a Greener Planet.* Harper and Row, 1990.

Lutz, Chuck. *Farming the Lord's Land: Christian Perspectives on American Agriculture.* Minneapolis: Augsburg, 1980.

McDonagh, Sean. *The Care for the Earth: A Call to a New Theology.* Santa Fe: Bear & Company, c. 1986.

Moltman, Jurgen. *God in Creation,* San Francisco: Harper & Row, Publishers, 1985.

Reed, Gerard. *Holy His Land: Caring for Creation.* Manuscript   San Diego, CA: Point Loma Nazarene College, 1990.

Rifkin, Jeremy, ed. *The Green Lifestyle Handbook: 1001 Ways You Can Heal the Earth.* New York: Henry Hold & Co., 1990.

Rolston, Holmes III. *Environmental Ethics: Duties to and Values in the Natural World.* Philadelphia: Temple University Press, 1988.

Schaeffer, Francis. *Pollution and the Death of Man: The Christian View of Ecology.* Tyndale House Publishers, 1970.

Schumacher, E.F. *Small is Beautiful: Economics as if People Mattered.* Harper and Row, 1973.

Sider, Ronald. *Rich Christians in a Hungry World,* Intervarsity Press, 1984.

Sombke, Laurence. *The Solution to Pollution.* Mastermedia Ltd., 1990.

Stadler, John ed. *Eco-Fiction.* Simon and Schuster, Inc., 1971.

Storer, John H. *The Web of Life,* The New American Library, 1953.

Wilkinson, Loren, ed. *Earthkeeping: Christian Stewardship of Natural Resources.* Grand Rapids: Eerdman's, 1980.

This list gives some examples of the many excellent, informative books now available to help you understand the environmental crisis and help you determine what you can do to help. Check at your library or bookstore. Some are theological studies of the issue; some are practical, get-down-to-business handbooks, and others are collections of essays.

If your eye is pure
there will be sunshine in your soul.

Matthew 6:22

If you would like more copies of
The Earth is the Lord's: Handle with Care--

_____ copies at $6.95 per copy

_____plus $1.00 postage and handling per book

_____Total for books

COTTON CANVAS GROCERY BAGS
Sturdy cotton canvas bags are perfect for groceries or gifts. Featuring an original hand-stenciled design by Sue Hurst,   "The Earth is the Lord's: Handle with Care" is inscribed on the bag in rich tones of green and blue. 16" by 12" by 7". Hand washable.

_____ bags at $9.95 per bag

_____shipping $1.00 per bag.

_____Total for bags

Name:_____

Address:_____

_____

_____Total enclosed (check or money order)

Send orders to:
Accord Publishing House
P.O. Box 582   Napoleon, Ohio 43545
(419) 267-3367
Thank you!

Estrella K. Danielle

GUÍA PRÁCTICA DE
masajes
para tu
pareja

imaginador

Estrella K. Danielle
Guía práctica de masajes para tu pareja. - 1ª. ed.-
Buenos Aires: Grupo Imaginador de Ediciones, 2006
96 p.; 20x14 cm.

ISBN: 950-768-567-7

1. Autoayuda. I. Título
CDD 158.1

Primera edición: octubre de 2006
Última reimpresión: diciembre de 2006

I.S.B.N.10: 950-768-567-7
I.S.B.N.13: 978-950-768-567-5

Se ha hecho el depósito que establece la Ley 11.723
© GIDESA, 2006
Bartolomé Mitre 3749 - Ciudad Autónoma de Buenos Aires
República Argentina
Impreso en Argentina - Printed in Argentina

Se terminó de imprimir en Mundo Gráfico S.R.L., Zeballos 885, Avellaneda,
en diciembre de 2006 con una tirada de 2.000 ejemplares.

INTRODUCCIÓN

Igual que un niño pequeño

El masaje es un acto instintivo y para comprobarlo sólo hace falta que observes, por ejemplo, a un niño pequeño, tan pequeño que aún no ha aprendido a hablar.

Cuando siente dolor su primera reacción es llorar, pues es su único modo, por ahora, de comunicarse. Pero, además, casi inmediatamente lleva una de sus manos a la zona donde siente dolor, para tocarla y aliviarla.

Así como los animales lamen sus propias heridas para que cicatricen, es sumamente probable que el hombre, en la antigüedad, cuando era puro instinto, tocara aquella zona de su cuerpo lastimada o dolorida.

Podemos afirmar, entonces, que el masaje es inherente a la condición humana y que ha sido, fue y será una herramienta terapéutica imprescindible.

Volver a los orígenes

En la actualidad hombres y mujeres han perdido gran parte de su capacidad instintiva. Los condicionamientos sociales y culturales hacen que muchas reacciones o acciones que tienen que ver con expresiones físicas ante determinados estímulos sean reprimidas y censuradas, y esto sucede sin que nos demos cuenta, es decir, ya no como acto consciente. El contacto con el propio cuerpo queda relegado a muy contados momentos, por lo general, íntimos.

De nosotros depende retomar el contacto corporal a través del masaje, y lograr que ocupe un lugar importante en nuestra vida. En relación con la pareja, específicamente, el acto del masaje es un excelente aliado para aumentar la comunicación.

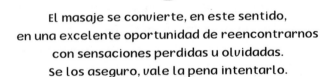

El masaje se convierte, en este sentido,
en una excelente oportunidad de reencontrarnos
con sensaciones perdidas u olvidadas.
Se los aseguro, vale la pena intentarlo.

Sin temor a equivocarme, puedo afirmar que el masaje es el lenguaje del que se vale nuestro cuerpo para expresarse. Es a través del masaje —dándolo y recibiéndolo— que experimentamos sensaciones y enviamos mensajes, muchas veces imposibles de expresar con palabras.

De simple acto instintivo, el hecho de tocar el cuerpo con las manos se sistematizó hasta convertirse en método; y de este modo surgió el masaje como técnica, como disciplina, tal como lo conocemos en la actualidad.

A pesar de que existen testimonios de que se trata de una disciplina muy antigua, la palabra "masaje" es relativamente nueva: proviene del árabe *masah*, cuyo significado es "frotar con la mano".

Nuestro objetivo

En las páginas de este libro hallarás una primera parte con nociones teóricas sobre el masaje: su desarrollo a través de la historia y de las diversas culturas que lo adoptaron o lo vieron surgir; las diversas clasificaciones que se practican en la actualidad (masaje shiatsu, sueco, tailandés, etcétera). A continuación, lo que consideraríamos la segunda parte, práctica, del libro, con toda la información y las instrucciones necesarias para llevar adelante una sesión completa de masaje relajante, diseñada especialmente para parejas.

Finalmente, un dossier sobre aceites esenciales, los mejores aliados para lograr una relajación completa. Describimos sus ventajas y su forma de aplicación en el masaje y en otras instancias.

el masaje

A TRAVÉS DEL TIEMPO Y LAS CULTURAS

el masaje
EN LAS CULTURAS ANTIGUAS

En China, el origen

De todos los testimonios que dan cuenta de la existencia del masaje como aliado terapéutico, el más antiguo ha sido hallado en China y se lo supone datado en el año 2700 a.C. Es un tratado de medicina cuya autoría se atribuye al emperador Huang Ti, de la Dinastía Amarilla, y su título es Nei Ching.

En una de sus páginas puede leerse: "friccionarse con la palma de la mano cada mañana, al levantarse, cuando la sangre y los humores están sosegados y quietos, protege de los resfriados, mantiene flexibles los órganos y evita pequeñas dolencias".

El masaje entre griegos y latinos

Galeno (131–210), un médico que prestaba sus servicios a la nobleza del Imperio Romano, elaboró y redactó nada menos que dieciséis tratados que describían las virtudes del masaje y el ejercicio físico, y muchos de los conceptos de su autoría tienen vigencia en la actualidad.

Galeno planteaba que había tres tipos de masaje, clasificados según su intensidad en "suave", "moderado" y "firme", pero hacía hincapié en que, independientemente de esta organización, las fricciones y los movimientos de las manos tenían que ser variados pues las fibras musculares debían frotarse en todas las direcciones posibles.

En uno de los tratados médicos de Galeno se hace referencia al hecho de que a los gladiadores romanos se les suministraban masajes en el cuerpo antes y después de una contienda. "Los ungen con aceite y friegan hasta que la piel se les pone roja", puede leerse en una de las páginas.

Tanto los griegos como los latinos ponían el acento en los beneficios de la realización del masaje después del baño, antes y después de la práctica de ejercicio físico y como recurso terapéutico ante la aparición de trastornos digestivos, respiratorios e, incluso, de índole anímico, como la melancolía.

Se sabe, además, que el gran conquistador romano Julio César recibía, todos los días, una reparadora sesión de masaje —que hasta incluía pellizcos— para aliviar su dolor crónico de cabeza.

> Plinio recurría también al masaje para aliviar
> los accesos de asma de los que era víctima.
> Quien se los suministraba, un extranjero, fue premiado
> por el emperador con la ciudadanía romana,
> uno de los más altos honores de la época.

De la Edad Media al Renacimiento

La práctica del masaje fue evolucionando con el correr de los siglos, hasta el comienzo de la Edad Media, una época caracterizada por el rechazo y la censura de todo lo relacionado con el contacto físico y el placer corporal, que supuso un freno al desarrollo de esta práctica.

> La doctrina cristiana de aquella época,
> férrea y dogmática, influyó para que el masaje
> fuera despreciado como herramienta útil
> para el bienestar físico y el goce.

Fue recién con el Renacimiento que el masaje recobró su prestigio perdido, y lo mismo sucedió con las artes y las ciencias. Se retomaron los estudios de los antiguos chinos, griegos y romanos y el arte de aliviar por medio del contacto de las manos con el cuerpo siguió desarrollándose, hasta nuestros días.

el masaje
EN LA ACTUALIDAD

En las últimas décadas, el masaje ha ido perfeccionándose y enriqueciéndose con el aporte de técnicas modernas. El objetivo sigue siendo el que guiaba a sus iniciadores: obtener un mayor bienestar y una mejor calidad de vida, y hacer un importante aporte a la salud.

Hoy en día podemos hablar de diversos tipos de masaje. Conozcamos los principales.

Shiatsu

El shiatsu es una técnica terapéutica de origen japonés que consiste en ejercer presión tanto con los dedos como con la palma de la mano, el codo, antebrazos, rodillas y pies, sobre diferentes zonas del cuerpo, consideradas vitales para el adecuado funcionamiento del organismo.

La palabra Shiatsu deriva de la combinación
de dos vocablos japoneses: *shi* y *atsu*.
Shi significa "dedo" y atsu, "presión".

Como resultado de esta presión intencional se logra activar la circulación sanguínea para relajar al paciente y, de este modo, prevenir o tratar diversas dolencias.

El beneficio conseguido a través de esta técnica no sólo abarca el nivel físico del individuo sino, también, el nivel emocional y espiritual.

El Zen shiatsu, uno de los estilos más destacados del shiatsu tradicional, incorpora, además de los mecanismos de presión mencionados, una serie de manipulaciones del cuerpo como estiramientos, levantamientos, fricciones, rodamientos, así como rotaciones de las articulaciones, los que, en conjunto, otorgan un bienestar psicofísico más profundo.

Un conocimiento básico del shiatsu favorecerá, además, la relación con la pareja, debido a que la aplicación de esta técnica activa los centros de placer, elevando el nivel de recepción sensitiva en forma considerable.

Masaje tailandés

El masaje tailandés consiste en la aplicación, sobre el cuerpo, de compresión y estiramientos, acompañados por balanceos suaves, rítmicos y constantes.

Los objetivos a los que apunta esta técnica son la reducción y el alivio de las tensiones musculares, la estimulación de la circulación, la optimización del funcionamiento del metabolismo en general, la recuperación del equilibrio interno (físico y mental), y la obtención de un estado de relajación y calma.

Originalmente, esta técnica se encontraba asociada a la práctica del budismo, y su fin consistía en actuar como un agente de meditación para la obtención del equilibrio y la unidad psicofísica y espiritual del individuo.

Si bien en Occidente el masaje tailandés es poco conocido, es ampliamente utilizado en el sudeste de Asia como prevención y curación de dolencias y enfermedades, así como una eficaz herramienta para la obtención del equilibrio psicofísico.

> El término tailandés *Nuad* significa "tocar con la intención de aliviar o curar", mientras que *Bo-Rarn*, término que deriva del sánscrito "purana", refiere a "algo sagrado, antiguo y reverenciado".

Masaje sueco

El masaje sueco es uno de los más difundidos en Occidente. Esta técnica fue desarrollada por un instructor de gimnasia y esgrima de nacionalidad sueca, llamado Per Henrik Ling (1776-1839), quien, en 1813, fundó el Instituto de Gimnasia Central Real en el que se practicaban dos técnicas que, con posterioridad, se combinaron y dieron origen al llamado "masaje sueco". Estas dos técnicas fueron la "cura sueca por movimiento" y la "gimnasia médica", que incluían tanto masajes como ejercicios físicos.

Recién a fines del siglo XX, el masaje sueco se introdujo en Estados Unidos, país en el que se popularizó y desde el que se difundió hacia diversas regiones del mundo.

Esta técnica consiste en la aplicación de movimientos activos y pasivos sobre el cuerpo del paciente, los que siempre se realizan en contra de la circulación sanguínea, es decir, llevando el masaje en dirección al corazón.

En el masaje sueco se utilizan aceites, previamente entibiados, para lograr un mejor contacto con la piel de la persona a tratar, y evitar, a la vez, cualquier tipo de fricción en la aplicación de la técnica.

Con el masaje sueco se busca mejorar la circulación sanguínea, relajar y tonificar la musculatura, aliviar los dolores articulares, estimular el sistema nervioso, reducir el estrés, atenuar los síntomas y dolores producidos por lumbago y ciática, así como relajar y purificar la piel.

Para ello, se sirve de determinados movimientos básicos que pueden aplicarse en forma individual o combinada, de acuerdo con la necesidad específica de cada paciente.

Los siguientes, son los movimientos básicos del masaje sueco:

EFFLEURAGE

Se aplican movimientos a lo largo del cuerpo en dirección al corazón. En general, se utiliza al inicio de la sesión para permitir que la persona a tratar se familiarice con el masaje en forma paulatina. Este movimiento permite que el cuerpo adquiera la temperatura y la relajación adecuadas para continuar con el resto de la sesión.

PETRISSAGE

Este movimiento consiste en "amasar" el cuerpo del paciente para activar la circulación sanguínea y lograr una profunda relajación general.

PRESIÓN DE PUNTOS

Consiste en presionar, con los dedos pulgar, los puntos de dolor que se manifiestan en el cuerpo, debido a la excesiva acumulación de tensión producto de situaciones de estrés psicofísico. Al presionar esos puntos de dolor, se produce la distensión del área afectada permitiendo una mayor relajación.

FRICCIÓN GENERALIZADA

Se fricciona el cuerpo en su totalidad con movimientos circulares, acentuando el movimiento en las zonas más afectadas. El objetivo básico de la fricción es el alivio de la tensión corporal.

◎ RODILLOS

Consiste en pellizcar, muy suavemente y como si se estuviera envolviendo sobre sí misma, la piel del paciente en áreas pequeñas y localizadas. Este movimiento provoca la distensión y activación de la zona tratada.

◎ TAPOTEMENT

Con las palmas de las manos cerradas, se aplican diversas "palmaditas" sobre la espalda del paciente y sobre los músculos más afectados, con el objetivo de activar la circulación energética del organismo. Generalmente, este movimiento se realiza en las últimas etapas de la sesión.

◎ CEPILLADO

Este movimiento se aplica al finalizar el masaje. Consiste en "cepillar" la totalidad del cuerpo deslizando, sobre él, la punta de los dedos. El movimiento debe ser suave y ejerciendo una leve presión para favorecer la relajación profunda y el alivio de las tensiones.

◎

Una sesión de masaje sueco puede durar, de acuerdo con las necesidades y limitaciones particulares de cada paciente, entre 30 y 90 minutos.

Masaje linfático

El masaje linfático es una técnica de estimulación manual que posee un objetivo particular: promover la adecuada circulación de la linfa en el organismo y, de esta manera, propiciar la eliminación de la mayor cantidad de toxinas que se encuentran acumuladas.

La linfa es una sustancia de consistencia lechosa que contiene linfocitos. Los linfocitos son un tipo de glóbulos blancos que tienen por función defender al organismo contra el ataque de agentes patógenos. Por lo tanto, los linfocitos, y así la linfa, resultan indispensables para el adecuado funcionamiento del sistema inmune del individuo.

Esta técnica consiste en aplicar masajes con los dedos y las manos sobre la totalidad del cuerpo. Como su fin principal es la estimulación del sistema linfático, el masaje debe ser muy suave y aplicado con movimientos circulares en las áreas en las que se ubican los nodos o puntos linfáticos.

El masaje se aplica, en primer lugar, en el rostro y en la mandíbula, por ser zonas que contienen gran cantidad de nodos linfáticos. Luego, se continúa por las axilas y, desde allí, a la totalidad del cuerpo.

Es importante tener en cuenta que este masaje activa los mecanismos de expulsión corporal (materia fecal, orina y sudor), los que pueden producirse con mayor frecuencia a la habitual; a la vez que favorece un descanso nocturno más profundo y relajado.

Más allá de la utilización del masaje linfático para todos los casos en los que se desee mejorar la circulación linfática y la eliminación de toxinas, esta técnica se aconseja en los siguientes casos:

- **Impotencia sexual (temporaria).**
- **Frigidez o falta de deseo sexual.**
- **Fatiga crónica.**
- **Debilidad general.**
- **Dolores premenstruales de consideración.**
- **Trastornos pre y postmenopáusicos.**

Este masaje puede ser complementado con otras técnicas, como shiatsu o masaje sueco.

Masaje watsu

El masaje watsu es una técnica particular que combina la esencia del masaje shiatsu y el ambiente acuático. Su creador fue Harold Dull, de nacionalidad estadounidense, quien, en 1980, fusionó el masaje shiatsu con diversas terapias que se realizan cuando la persona a tratar se encuentra sumergida en el agua.

Una de las características de esta técnica es que, a la vez que el paciente consigue una plena relajación corporal, también se energiza.

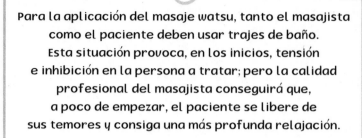

Para la aplicación del masaje watsu, tanto el masajista como el paciente deben usar trajes de baño. Esta situación provoca, en los inicios, tensión e inhibición en la persona a tratar; pero la calidad profesional del masajista conseguirá que, a poco de empezar, el paciente se libere de sus temores y consiga una más profunda relajación.

El masaje watsu se realiza en una piscina o medio similar. El agua debe estar tibia y cubrir, al paciente, hasta el pecho. En ese medio, además del masaje shiatsu, el masajista estimula a la persona a realizar movimientos espontáneos y flotar en libertad.

El ambiente acuático en el que se desarrolla la sesión, así como la calidez del agua y lo placentero de los masajes, propicia un medio excelente para la meditación y relajación profundas.

masaje relajante
PARA PAREJAS

ANTES DE **comenzar**

El ambiente adecuado

Debes buscar el lugar ideal para la realización de la sesión de masaje. Éste debería reunir ciertas características:

- **Ser silencioso.**
- **Tener una temperatura agradable.**
- **Ser cómodo (lo suficiente para poder movernos sin dificultad de un extremo al otro del cuerpo de nuestra pareja, mientras realizamos el masaje).**

Todo depende de las características del hogar... la cocina, si es amplia, es una opción que no debe despreciarse; el comedor, si haces a un lado la mesa y las sillas, puede resultar ideal; aunque no recomendaría el cuarto, ya que quizá esté muy relacionado mentalmente con el acto sexual, y el masaje es una cuestión diferente, cuyo objetivo es la distensión y la relajación.

La luz tenue: compañera del masaje

Las luces tenues invitan a la calma y la relajación. Haz lo posible para que el ambiente, sin llegar a las penumbras, tenga una iluminación "baja": lámparas veladoras ubicadas lejos del sitio exacto en el que tú y tu pareja se ubicarán para llevar a cabo la sesión, o una lámpara de pie convenientemente cubierta por un género de color.

Ah, no olvides las velas, pues son uno de los condimentos que más ayudan a la relajación. Hoy puedes conseguirlas en infinidad de formatos y colores, huecas o macizas, y hasta las hay delicadamente perfumadas.

No olvides los aromas

En cuanto al perfume, hay varias opciones: desde los aromáticos inciensos, pasando por las velas, hasta un cuenco con agua en la que floten varios jazmines.

Otra buena opción son los aceites aromáticos que emanan perfume cuando se calientan en hornos especiales. Ten en cuenta que los aromas delicados despiertan los sentidos, y aprovéchalos.

Por lo general, los sahumerios y los aceites se elaboran a partir de las mismas esencias. Por eso, a continuación te contamos cuáles son las más apropiadas para armonizar, proteger y relajar.

ALMIZCLE
Armoniza el ambiente y aleja las tensiones.

AZAHAR
Atrae la felicidad, la calma y aleja los pensamientos negativos.

CALÉNDULA
Una vez lograda la serenidad, esta esencia ayuda a conservarla.

EUCALIPTO
Aleja la agresividad y elimina tensiones.

FLOR DE AZAHAR
Propicia el entendimiento amoroso entre dos personas.

GERANIO
Es tranquilizante y armonizador del sistema nervioso.

INCIENSO
Transforma lo negativo en positivo.

LAVANDA
Calma los nervios y acrecienta el optimismo.

MADRESELVA
Alivia las tensiones físicas y suaviza el carácter.

MENTA
Favorece la respiración pausada y tranquila. Combate el cansancio y la tristeza.

MUSK
Estimula los sentimientos elevados como el amor y la amistad. Aleja las energías negativas.

NARDO
Ayuda a la relajación física y psíquica y colabora con el sueño reparador.

PACHULÍ
Incrementa las energías positivas y levanta el ánimo.

PINO
Atrae las vibraciones psíquicas positivas. Purifica los ambientes cargados de energía negativa.

ROSA
Otorga paz y armonía a la pareja.

SÁNDALO
Aleja del ambiente las energías y vibraciones negativas.

TILO
Relaja y descontractura el cuerpo y brinda paz interior.

La superficie ideal

La superficie sobre la que se acostará tu pareja debe ser dura, pero no hasta el punto de causar molestias. Una colchoneta delgada, o un par de mantas ubicadas sobre el piso o una mesa grande serán ideales. No recomiendo el colchón debido a que por su blandura hará que el cuerpo se hunda y no reaccione del todo a ciertas maniobras de la sesión de masaje.

> Mi preferida es una esterilla amplia,
> que coloco sobre una manta, en el piso.

Si quieres, puedes cubrir la colchoneta, las mantas o la esterilla con una sábana, pero debes tener en cuenta que la superficie se manchará al aplicar aceite sobre el cuerpo.

No olvides un almohadón no demasiado alto. Quizá alguno de los dos lo necesite para estar más cómodo, ubicándolo bajo la cabeza cuando esté boca arriba, o debajo de la pelvis cuando se acueste boca abajo.

Ten a mano otra sábana y una manta liviana. La relajación que provoca el masaje hace que la temperatura corporal descienda, y es probable que quien reciba el masaje sienta algo de frío.

Accesorios deliciosos

Es buena idea completar el equipo de accesorios para la sesión con una fuente de frutas frescas, de ésas que se comen de un mordisco, sin tener que recurrir a los cubiertos. Si a ti y a tu pareja les gusta el chocolate, consigan el mejor, en barra o bajo la forma de exquisitos bombones. Tengan al alcance de la mano, también, una bebida de su preferencia.

La idea es que estén cómodos y que nada interrumpa la sesión de masajes.

El uso del aceite

El aceite, además de lubricar y permitir que las manos se deslicen suavemente sobre la piel, reaviva los sentidos y es altamente excitante.

Los masajes que les propongo en este libro deben realizarse indefectiblemente con alguna clase de aceite. El modo correcto es volcar una pequeña cantidad en la palma de la mano, frotar ambas manos y aplicarlo en el cuerpo de la pareja, mientras se realiza el masaje.

El objetivo que buscamos al verter el aceite en la mano
y no directamente sobre el cuerpo es hacer que
se entibie con el frotamiento de ambas palmas.
Si lo volcáramos en el cuerpo, es probable que
a nuestra pareja no le resultara muy agradable.

El aceite, sea del tipo que sea, ayuda a que el masaje sea profundo, activa la circulación, revitaliza la piel y colabora con la regeneración celular de los tejidos, entre otras maravillosas ventajas. Además, evita que las manos de quien hace la maniobra friccionen la piel del cuerpo de quien la recibe, generando una sensación molesta y un resultado negativo de la maniobra del masaje.

Puedes optar por algún aceite esencial o, simplemente, por aceite neutro, como el que se utiliza para suavizar la delicada piel de los bebés.

Si deseas tener mayor información sobre este excelente aliado de los masajes relajantes, a partir de la página 62 hallarás un dossier con información sobre aceites esenciales, en el que encontrarás, entre otras nociones, claves para elegir el aceite más adecuado para el fin que deseas conseguir (estimular, relajar, distender, armonizar, etcétera) y una descripción de otros usos maravillosos del aceite en baños, compresas e inhalaciones, por ejemplo.

Disfruten de las imágenes que hallarán a continuación. Les enseñarán, paso a paso, la secuencia de una sesión de masaje relajante que los dejará listos para el placer. Verán que en algunos casos es ella quien le hace masajes a él, y viceversa, aunque la elección de quien haga el masaje es libre, y queda a criterio de ustedes.

SESIÓN DE

masajes

para tu
pareja

TÉCNICAS DE masaje

Roce suave

Utilizarán esta técnica para aplicar el aceite sobre el cuerpo. Se trata del primer contacto de las manos con la piel, y tiene una finalidad exploratoria.
Coloca las palmas de las manos planas, y deslízalas estableciendo el contacto.

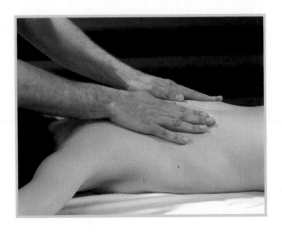

Estás "leyendo" en el cuerpo de tu pareja, sin palabras, sin explicaciones... tus manos y la piel. Nada más.

Amasamiento

Se trata del tipo de manipulación adecuada para las zonas con más musculatura del cuerpo, pues allí necesita establecerse un contacto más enérgico.
Mueve alternativamente las dos manos, como si una fuera hacia delante y la otra, hacia atrás.

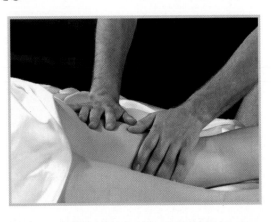

A lo largo de toda la sesión deberán emplear ciertas técnicas, que tienen que ver con la posición de las manos y el tipo de presión que ejercen sobre la piel de quien recibe el masaje.

Movimientos circulares

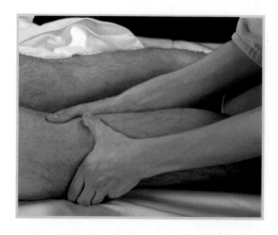

Con los dedos pulgares: trabajarás con la idea de "abrir" una zona, realizando movimientos circulares hacia fuera y hacia adentro.

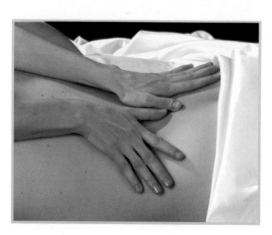

Con toda la mano: sigues con la idea de "abrir". La diferencia con el punto anterior radica en que trabajarás con la palma de la mano entera cuando se trate de zonas más amplias del cuerpo, como la espalda.

Roce suave
con los dedos

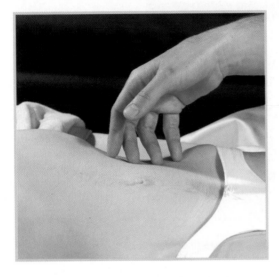

Sólo debes rozar delicadamente con los dedos, yendo
y viniendo. Es la técnica
adecuada para las zonas
más sensibles, como el rostro, el cabello, el pecho y el
vientre.

Suave, delicadamente,
tus dedos acarician.
Dan y reciben.

Los masajes que te proponemos en estas páginas son, esencialmente, relajantes y descontracturantes. Por eso, puedes recurrir a ellos cada vez que tú o tu pareja necesiten quitarse de encima las tensiones de un día difícil.

Presión

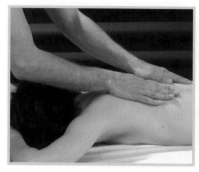

Trabajarás con toda la palma de la mano, o con el puño cerrado, para proporcionar una sensación intensa. La idea es presionar tratando de establecer contacto con la estructura ósea.

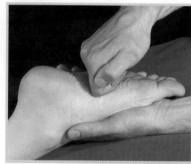

Arco radial

El arco radial de tu mano (la zona que va desde el índice hasta el pulgar) se apoya y recorre la pierna o el brazo, de arriba hacia abajo.

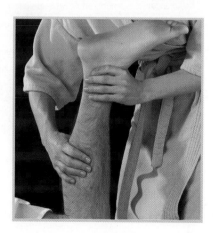

AL PRINCIPIO,
boca abajo

Mis manos en tu espalda

Para masajear la
espalda, quien da
el masaje se colocará
en la cabecera,
sentado sobre
los talones
o arrodillado.

PASO 1

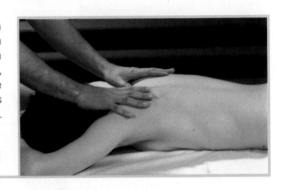

Los dedos pulgares rodean la séptima vértebra cervical (la
más sobresaliente), y dibujan círculos alrededor, hacia un
lado y hacia el otro, sin ejercer demasiada presión.

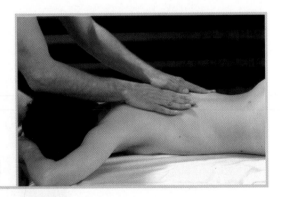

PASO 2

Las manos se deslizan por la espalda, a los costados de la
columna vertebral, desde los hombros y hasta llegar al sacro.

Quien recibe el masaje se acuesta boca abajo.
Quien lo da irá cambiando de posición de acuerdo
con la zona del cuerpo que le toque trabajar
en cada momento.

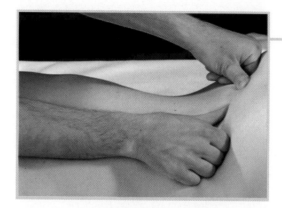

PASO 3

Los dedos pulgares de cada mano hacen presión sobre el sacro, y dibujan círculos, para relajar.

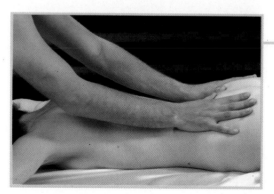

PASO 4

Ahora, son las palmas de las manos las que dibujan círculos sobre el sacro.

PASO 5

Con firmeza, apoyar los talones de las manos sobre los huesos de la cadera. Sin separarlos de la zona, mover los talones para que se mueva toda la cadera.

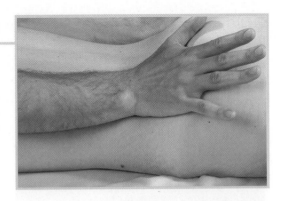

PASO 6

Desde los glúteos, abrazando la cintura, las manos suben por los costados de la espalda hasta llegar a los omóplatos.

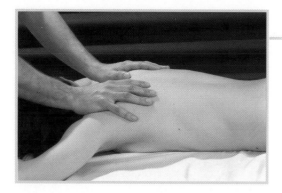

PASO 7

Las manos se apoyan sobre los omóplatos y ejercen una suave presión.

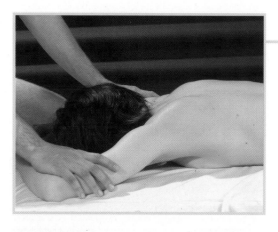

PASO 8

Las manos se deslizan por los brazos, hasta tocar las manos de quien recibe el masaje. La idea es arrastrar la tensión alojada en el cuerpo para que salga por las manos.

Repite toda la secuencia dos veces.
Comienza a hacerla una tercera vez,
pero con una diferencia: desde los omóplatos,
seguirás subiendo hasta el cuello, para realizar
el paso que te indico a continuación.

PASO 9

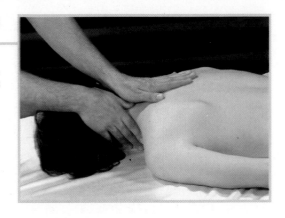

Las manos rodean el cuello, masajeando los músculos de la nuca y la cabeza.

Ahora, quien da el masaje cambiará de posición. Colócate de costado, mirando hacia la cabeza de tu compañero.
Para realizar los pasos que se indican a continuación, ten en cuenta que deberás dividir imaginariamente a la espalda en dos mitades, separadas por la columna vertebral.
Trabajarás primero una mitad, y luego la otra.

PASO 10

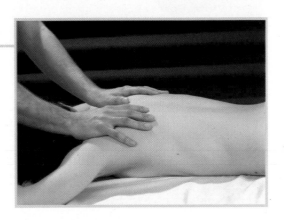

Una mano se coloca detrás de la otra, y ascienden juntas desde la cadera hacia el omóplato. Se separan de la espalda para volver a apoyarse en la cadera, y subir nuevamente, dos o tres veces.

PASO 11

Una mano sujeta al hombro, y la otra rodea el omóplato.

La mano recorre todos los bordes del omóplato: el interno, el superior y el externo.

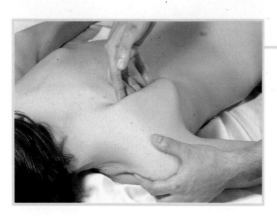

PASO 12

Toma el hombro de modo que se marque el omóplato y, con la otra mano, despega el borde interno del omóplato.

PASO 13

Toma el hombro con una mano y, con el pulgar y el índice de la otra, rodea la punta del omóplato. Haz que el omóplato se desplace haciendo pequeños movimientos ascendentes y descendentes.

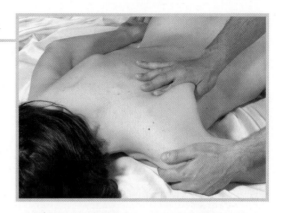

PASO 14

Cambia la posición de las manos: la que sujetaba el hombro es la que va a trabajar ahora. Con la otra mano, sujeta el brazo, y masajea con la mano libre los músculos que van desde el hombro hacia el cuello.

En tus brazos...

La persona que hace el masaje se sienta al costado
de quien lo recibe, mirando hacia la cabecera.

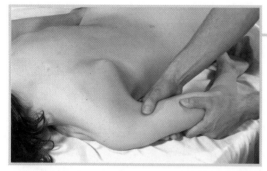

PASO 15

Desliza las manos por el
brazo y el antebrazo. Debes
rodear el brazo y amasar los
músculos con movimientos
circulares.

PASO 16

Toma la mano con las tuyas
y, con los dedos pulgares,
realiza movimientos circulares en toda la palma.

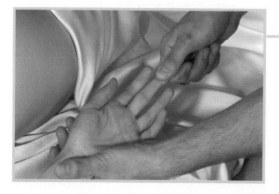

PASO 17

Toma cada dedo y haz con
ellos movimientos circulares hacia un lado y hacia el
otro. Luego, estira cada dedo como si quisieras des-
pegarlo de la mano.

Mis manos en tus piernas

Para masajear las piernas, quien da el masaje se sentará sobre sus talones o se arrodillará a los pies de quien lo recibe.

PASO 18

Apoya una mano detrás de la otra, en la cara posterior de la pierna, y haz trayectos largos, desde el tobillo hasta el muslo, sin despegar las palmas de la piel. Repítelo tres o cuatro veces, colocando aceite cuando haga falta.

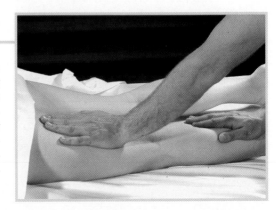

PASO 19

Las palmas de las dos manos rodean el muslo y masajean la zona con movimientos circulares.

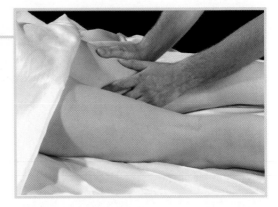

PASO 20

Una mano va, y la otra viene... hacia adentro y hacia fuera, como amasando todos los músculos del muslo.

Detente donde notes tensión y masajea especialmente esa zona, hasta relajarla por completo.

PASO 21

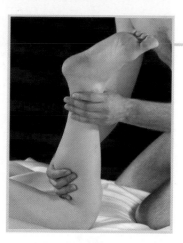

Apoya las manos sobre el hueco de la rodilla y ejerce una suave presión, para que tu pareja sienta el contacto con las articulaciones.

PASO 22

Flexiona la pierna de tu pareja, y mantenla sujeta con una de tus manos, a la altura del tobillo. Tu otra mano se apoya sobre los músculos de la pantorrilla y va presionando y soltando, desde la rodilla hasta el tobillo, con el arco radial. Repítelo tres o cuatro veces.

PASO 23

El tobillo se moviliza, estirando la punta del pie hacia arriba y luego llevando hacia arriba el talón, alternativamente.
A continuación, las manos hacen que el pie describa movimientos circulares, para relajar.

PASO 24

Acentúa la flexión de la rodilla llevando el talón al glúteo. Realiza una presión suave y, unos momentos después, suelta y estira la pierna.

Estoy a tus pies

Quien da el masaje debe sentarse a los pies de quien lo recibe,
y apoyar el pie a trabajar sobre un almohadón.

PASO 25

Las dos manos toman el pie
y los pulgares masajean en
forma circular el talón.

PASO 26

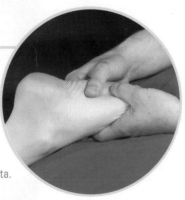

En la misma posición, los pulgares masajean ahora la zona media del pie y el metatarso, es decir,
la almohadilla que está ubicada justo antes del
nacimiento de los dedos.

Luego trabaja con cada dedo del pie, movi-
lizándolo hacia un lado y hacia otro. Estira
cada dedo desde su nacimiento hacia la punta.

PASO 27

Con el puño de tu mano,
ejerce presión en toda la
planta del pie.

Mis manos en tus piernas

Para masajear las piernas, quien da el masaje se sentará sobre los talones o se arrodillará a los pies de quien lo recibe.

PASO 28

La manos se apoyan, una a continuación de la otra, sobre las piernas. Se deslizan desde abajo hacia arriba, varias veces.

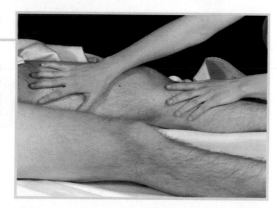

PASO 29

Las manos se deslizan desde el muslo hacia la ingle, suavemente.

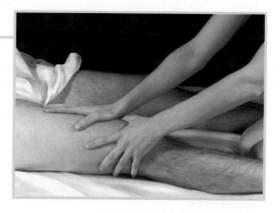

50

Quien recibe el masaje se acuesta boca arriba. Quien lo da irá cambiando de posición de acuerdo con la zona del cuerpo que le toque trabajar en cada momento.

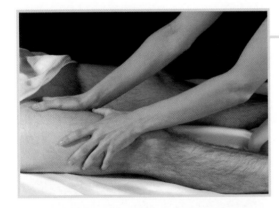

PASO 30

Las palmas de las manos, apoyadas sobre el muslo, hacen movimientos circulares profundos, para actuar sobre los músculos.

PASO 31

Las manos rodean el muslo y suben desde la rodilla hasta la ingle, y luego bajan. Repite el movimiento tres o cuatro veces.

PASO 32

Una detrás de la otra, las palmas de las manos se apoyan en el tobillo y suben y bajan hacia y desde la rodilla.

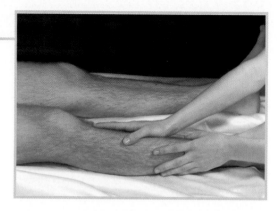

PASO 33

Los pulgares de los dedos masajean el empeine con movimientos circulares. Luego, partiendo desde el tobillo, recorren el empeine hasta terminar en la punta de cada dedo del pie.

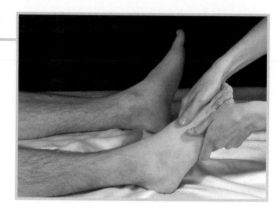

PASO 34

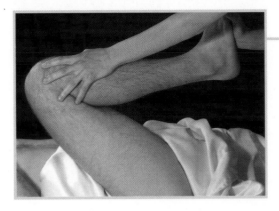

Una de tus manos toma el pie de tu pareja y la otra se apoya en la rodilla. Haz que la pierna se flexione acercando el muslo al vientre. Sostén la presión, mientras le pides a tu pareja que respire profundamente.

PASO 35

Apoya una mano en la cara externa de la rodilla y la otra, en el costado del muslo. Empuja para que la pierna flexionada cruce sobre la otra, que permanece extendida.

Lo que estás haciendo es provocar una torsión de la columna, para relajar y aliviar la tensión.

PASO 36

Una de tus manos se apoya debajo de la rodilla, y la otra sujeta la pierna a la altura del tobillo. Practica un suave tirón de la pierna hacia tu cuerpo.

En tu vientre...

Quien da el masaje se sienta al costado de quien lo recibe, y se arrodilla, de ser necesario, para trabajar sobre la zona.

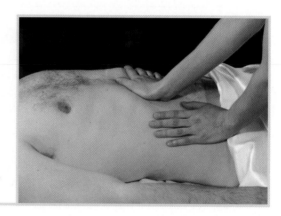

PASO 37

Tus manos están siguiendo el recorrido del intestino grueso, relajando los músculos del abdomen.

Apoya una mano detrás de la otra sobre el vientre de tu pareja y deslízalas en forma circular, suavemente. Comienza por el costado derecho, asciende, trabaja en forma transversal —debajo de las costillas— y desciende por el costado izquierdo. Repite tres o cuatro veces.

No olvides que el broche de oro en una buena sesión de masajes es un baño de inmersión, que los relajará aún más, o una ducha vigorizante. Pruébalo y verás lo bien que te sientes.

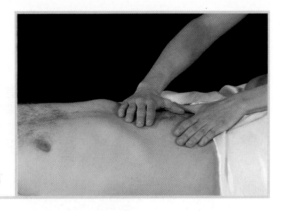

PASO 38

Las palmas de las manos dibujan círculos alrededor del ombligo, justo sobre el lugar donde está ubicado el intestino delgado.

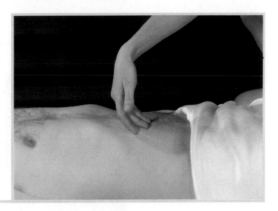

PASO 39

Ahora, una delicadísima caricia de tus dedos, que van y vienen sobre el vientre de tu pareja, relajándolo.

Mis manos en tu pecho

Quien da el masaje se colocará arrodillado o sentado
sobre los talones, en la cabecera.

PASO 40

Ambas manos se apoyan sobre el pecho y se deslizan hacia los hombros, varias veces.

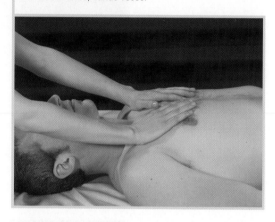

Puedes alternar el movimiento de las manos, trabajando primero con una y luego con la otra.

PASO 41

Apoya los talones de las manos sobre los hombros, y
ejerce presión con la idea de
que los hombros se hundan.

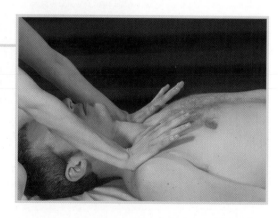

PASO 42

Desliza las manos por los brazos, hasta donde llegues, es decir, hasta donde tu posición te lo permita.

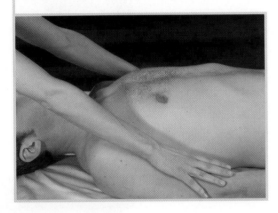

PASO 43

Ahora, las manos toman los brazos pero por debajo, y van subiendo hacia los hombros.

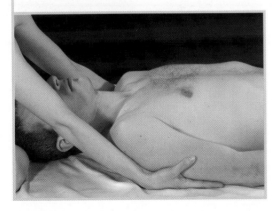

PASO 44

Las manos llegan hasta los hombros y los despegan de la superficie, con suavidad.

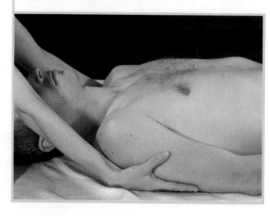

PASO 45

Rodea el cuello de tu pareja con ambas manos y deslízalas hacia fuera.

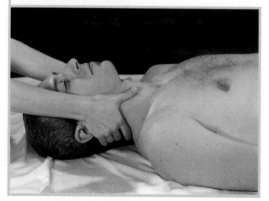

Te sugiero que repitas toda la secuencia (pasos 40 a 45 inclusive) unas tres veces, para producir un efecto profundo de alivio y distensión.

PASO 46

Sostén el cuello de tu pareja con ambas manos y haz que gire la cabeza hacia uno y otro costado. Mientras esto sucede, el dedo pulgar masajea con movimientos circulares los músculos del costado del cuello.

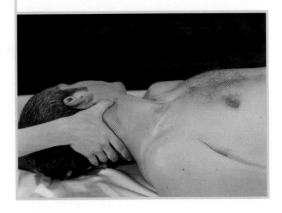

PASO 47

Las manos se deslizan desde la nuca hacia la coronilla, levantando la cabeza para acercar el mentón al pecho.

Haz que la cabeza se eleve lentamente, para producir el estiramiento profundo de los músculos del cuello.

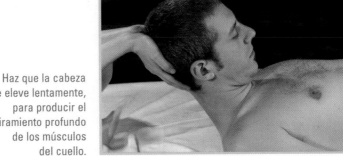

Descubriendo tu rostro

La posición es igual a la descripta en la secuencia anterior.

PASO 48

Desliza tus dedos pulgares sobre la frente de tu pareja, desde el centro hacia las sienes, con la intención de despejar y descongestionar la zona.

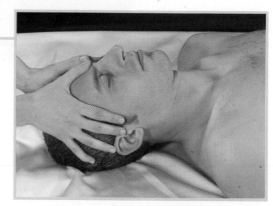

PASO 49

Apoya las yemas de los dedos sobre los pómulos, y haz que se movilicen arrastrando con ellas la piel, como si intentaras despegarla.

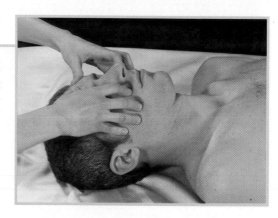

Las yemas de tus dedos pueden recorrer el mentón, la zona alrededor de los ojos y el punto de articulación de las mandíbulas, siempre en forma suave... casi como una caricia.

PASO 50

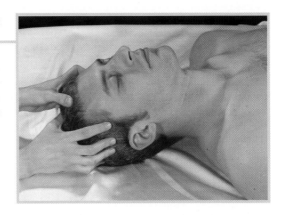

Masajea el cuero cabelludo como si estuvieras lavándole el cabello. Trabaja con la intención de que la piel se despegue del cráneo.

DOSSIER SOBRE TÉCNICAS DE
relajación

Relajación exprés
con aceites esenciales

Para realizar las técnicas de relajación que describimos a continuación sólo deberás aplicar unas gotas del aceite elegido sobre tus manos y frotarlas.
Repite la aplicación del aceite tantas veces como sea necesario: tus manos siempre deberán estar humectadas para evitar la fricción.

RELAJACIÓN PARA EL ROSTRO

• Con las manos untadas en el aceite, comienza la aplicación por la frente con movimientos circulares.
Continúa masajeando las sienes, sigue por la nariz y luego dirígete hacia los pómulos: allí trabajarás con movimientos circulares hacia fuera, es decir, hacia las orejas.
Finalmente bordea los labios y termina en el mentón y el cuello.

• Comienza a masajear más profundamente cada una de las partes recién mencionadas, haciendo hincapié en los costados de la nariz y el borde superior del labio.

• Deja penetrar el aceite durante diez minutos. Transcurrido este tiempo, la piel debería haber absorbido todo el aceite. Si no es así, y han quedado residuos, puedes quitarlos del rostro con un paño suave.

Durante los diez minutos en que dejas que penetre el aceite puedes continuar haciendo masajes en el rostro, pero en forma muy suave.

Los aceites esenciales son los mejores aliados para lograr una relajación profunda pero, además, existen ciertas técnicas relacionadas con la meditación y la visualización que les serán de gran ayuda.

RELAJACIÓN PARA EL CUELLO Y LOS HOMBROS

• Con las manos untadas en el aceite, comienza la aplicación bajo el mentón, dirigiéndote hacia el pecho, con movimientos suaves de todos los dedos de las manos.

• Realiza el mismo procedimiento pero ahora comenzando bajo la nuca, y dirigiéndote hacia la espalda. Trabaja con ambas manos llevando el aceite hacia los hombros.

• Redondea los hombros ejerciendo presión con las manos y deja actuar el aceite diez minutos, para que penetre en la piel.

RELAJACIÓN PARA PECHO Y ABDOMEN

La zona del abdomen es muy sensible. Trabaja con suavidad hasta que sientas que se ha relajado y luego deja que el aceite penetre en la piel.

• Comienza acariciando el pecho suavemente desde las clavículas. La presión que ejerces debe ser muy leve y debes trabajar en forma de círculos, siempre en el sentido de las agujas del reloj.

• Una vez que sientas que la zona del pecho se ha relajado comienza a trabajar sobre el abdomen, también con movimientos circulares.

RELAJACIÓN PARA PIES Y PIERNAS

• Trabaja con ambas manos, rodeando el muslo desde su inicio, como abrazándolo. Deberás ir descendiendo hasta llegar a las rodillas.

• Vuelve a colocar aceite en tus manos y sigue trabajando del mismo modo, desde las rodillas hasta el tobillo. Masajea muy bien cada tobillo y los empeines, pues allí se alojan muchas tensiones.

• Finaliza masajeando suavemente las plantas de los pies y cada uno de los dedos. Detente en cada uno de ellos con los dedos pulgares de tu mano, estirándolos y haciendo suaves rotaciones.

RELAJACIÓN PARA EL CUERO CABELLUDO

• Aplica unas gotas de aceite solamente en las yemas de tus dedos y comienza a masajear con movimientos circulares la parte trasera de la cabeza, desde la nuca hasta llegar a la frente.

• Frota todo el cuero cabelludo con la yema de los dedos ejerciendo una presión moderada.

• Masajea, esta vez suavemente, los laterales, dirigiéndote hacia las sienes.

• Finaliza con un masaje completo, que abarque toda la superficie del cuero cabelludo.

A partir de la página 75 de este libro hallarás toda la información necesaria para saber cuáles son los aceites ideales para relajar y descontracturar.
Además, te brindamos todas las claves para descubrir otros usos maravillosos de los aceites.

paso a paso
DE A DOS

A continuación hallarás la descripción sintética de la sesión de masaje relajante para parejas que acabas de ver en fotografías, en las páginas a color de este libro.

Ten en cuenta que la sesión vale tanto para ser ejecutada sobre el cuerpo de un hombre como sobre el de una mujer. En este sentido, los masajes que proponemos no tocan puntos específicos del cuerpo de uno u otro sexo, sino que buscan relajar y estimular zonas generales, con el fin de descontracturarlas y aliviar las tensiones.

No olvides acondicionar el ambiente donde tendrá
lugar la sesión de masaje como se indicó anteriormente.
Ten cuidado con la temperatura: cuando
los cuerpos se relajan suele sentirse frío.
Ah, y aplica tanto aceite como sea necesario,
sin escatimar.

Técnicas de masaje

ROCE SUAVE

Las palmas de las manos se deslizan con suavidad, estableciendo un contacto leve con el cuerpo.

AMASAMIENTO

Las palmas de las manos amasan, imprimiendo una presión mediana, con la intención de trabajar la musculatura.

MOVIMIENTOS CIRCULARES

Con los dedos pulgares: se trabaja con la intención de "abrir" determinadas zonas, ejerciendo presión mediana.

Con la palma de las manos: adecuado para trabajar zonas más grandes del cuerpo.

ROCE SUAVE CON LOS DEDOS

Los dedos acarician suavemente las zonas más sensibles del cuerpo (glúteos, vientre, rostro).

PRESIÓN

Con la palma de la mano o con el puño cerrado —según la zona a masajear—, se establece un contacto intenso, presionando con firmeza, con la intención de llegar hasta la estructura ósea.

⊚ ARCO RADIAL

Se aplica sobre el cuerpo —el brazo o la pantorrilla— el arco radial de la mano, es decir, la zona ubicada entre el índice y el pulgar.

Masaje sobre la cara anterior del cuerpo

La espalda

1 Movimientos circulares con los pulgares alrededor de la séptima vértebra (la más sobresaliente).

2 Roce suave de las manos a los costados de la columna, desde los hombros y hasta el sacro.

3 Movimientos circulares con los pulgares sobre la zona del sacro.

4 Movimientos circulares con las palmas de las manos, sobre la zona del sacro.

5 Presión con los talones de las manos sobre los huesos de la cadera.

6 Roce suave de las palmas de las manos, desde la cintura y ascendiendo por los costados de la espalda hasta llegar a los omóplatos.

7 Presión de las palmas de las manos sobre los omóplatos.

8 Roce suave de las palmas de las manos en los brazos, desde los hombros hasta las manos.

9 Masaje de presión mediana con las palmas de las manos, sobre el cuello, la nuca y la cabeza.

10 Deslizamiento de las palmas de las manos desde la cadera hasta el omóplato.

11 Masaje sobre el omóplato, recorriendo su contorno con la palma de una mano mientras la otra sujeta el hombro.

12 Despegue del omóplato sosteniendo el hombro con una mano.

13 Desplazamiento ascendente y descendente del omóplato tomando el hombro con una mano y asiendo la punta del omóplato con el dedo pulgar y el dedo índice.

14 Masaje de presión mediana sobre los músculos que van desde el hombro hasta el cuello, sosteniendo el brazo con una de las manos.

Los brazos

15 Amasamiento de los músculos de brazo y antebrazo, con movimientos circulares.

16 Movimientos circulares de los dedos pulgares en la palma de la mano.

17 Rotación de cada dedo, y estiramiento, con la intención de "separarlo" de la mano.

Las piernas

18 Deslizamiento con presión mediana de las palmas de las manos en la cara posterior de la pierna, desde el tobillo hasta el muslo.

19 Movimientos circulares de las palmas de las manos sobre el muslo.

20 Amasamiento de los músculos del muslo.

21 Presión mediana sobre el hueco de la rodilla.

22 Masaje con el arco radial de la mano sobre la pantorrilla, presionando y soltando, desde la rodilla hasta el tobillo.

23 Movilización del tobillo. En primer lugar, llevando la punta del pie y el talón hacia arriba, alternativamente. En segundo lugar, haciendo que el tobillo rote hacia un lado y hacia el otro.

24 Estiramiento muscular llevando la pierna flexionada hacia atrás, con la intención de que el talón toque el glúteo.

Los pies

25 Movimientos circulares con los dedos pulgares sobre el talón del pie.

26 Movimientos circulares con los dedos pulgares sobre la zona media del pie y el metatarso (la almohadilla ubicada debajo del nacimiento de los dedos).

27 Presión intensa del talón de la mano sobre toda la planta del pie.

Masaje sobre la cara posterior del cuerpo

Las piernas

28 Deslizamiento de las palmas de las manos, desde abajo hacia arriba, sobre la pierna.

29 Deslizamiento de las palmas de las manos desde el muslo hacia la ingle.

30 Movimientos circulares con presión intensa de las palmas de las manos sobre los muslos, para actuar sobre los músculos.

31 Amasamiento del muslo, desde la rodilla hacia la ingle, con presión mediana y movimiento ascendente y descendente.

32 Deslizamiento con presión mediana de las palmas de las manos sobre la pantorrilla, bajando y subiendo desde el tobillo y hacia la rodilla.

33 Movimientos circulares con los dedos pulgares sobre el empeine. Deslizamiento de los pulgares desde el tobillo, recorriendo el empeine hasta terminar en la punta de cada dedo del pie.

34 Estiramiento de los músculos ejerciendo presión sobre la pierna flexionada, con la idea de que el muslo toque el vientre.

35 Estiramiento de los músculos ejerciendo presión sobre la pierna flexionada, para cruzarla sobre la otra, que permanece extendida. Además de estirar los músculos del muslo, el cruce de la pierna hace que se produzca torsión de la columna vertebral.

36 Suave tirón de la pierna tomándola con las manos, a la altura de la rodilla y del tobillo.

El vientre

37 Deslizamiento de las palmas de las manos, siguiendo el recorrido del intestino grueso (ascensión por el costado derecho, deslizamiento transversal debajo de las costillas, y descenso por el lado izquierdo.

38 Deslizamiento de las palmas de las manos en círculos alrededor del ombligo.

39 Roce suave de los dedos sobre el vientre.

El pecho

40 Deslizamiento de las palmas de las manos sobre el pecho, desde el centro y hasta los hombros.

41 Presión de intensidad mediana de los talones de las manos sobre los hombros, con la idea de hundirlos.

42 Deslizamiento suave de las palmas de las manos sobre los brazos, a partir del hombro y hacia las muñecas.

43 Deslizamiento de las manos por debajo de los hombros, a partir de las muñecas y hacia los hombros.

44 Despegue de los hombros, tomándolos con las manos, con movimiento lento y suave.

45 Deslizamiento de las palmas de las manos sobre el cuello, comenzando por el centro (debajo de la nuca) y hacia delante.

46 Rotación de la cabeza tomando el cuello con ambas manos, combinada con movimientos circulares de los pulgares en los músculos del costado del cuello.

47 Deslizamiento de las palmas de las manos a partir de la nuca y hacia la coronilla, levantando la cabeza con la idea de que el mentón toque el pecho.

El rostro

48 Deslizamiento de los dedos pulgares por la frente, desde el centro hasta las sienes.

49 Deslizamiento de las yemas de los dedos sobre los pómulos, con la intención de movilizar la piel, como si quisiera despegársela.

50 Masaje de presión mediana con las yemas de los dedos sobre el cuero cabelludo, con la intención de que la piel se despegue del cráneo.

dossier

EL PODER DE LOS ACEITES ESENCIALES

aromaterapia:
EL PODER DE LOS ACEITES

¿Qué es la aromaterapia?

La aromaterapia es uno de los métodos alternativos naturales que existen para aliviar trastornos y malestares.

No es una ciencia en el sentido estricto de la palabra, pero sí mantiene la categoría de terapia alternativa, como lo son también la gemoterapia, la colorterapia, la acupuntura, la reflexología, la homeopatía, etc., así como diversas técnicas terapéuticas muy en boga en nuestros días.

La aromaterapia se basa en la utilización de sustancias aromáticas naturales, que son los llamados aceites bases.

La aromaterapia, como toda terapia alternativa, propone un reencuentro con nuestra naturaleza perdida. Y nos ofrece el hermoso camino de los aromas para llegar a ella.

Extracción de los aceites esenciales

Los aceites básicos que se utilizan en aromaterapia son extraídos de las plantas. Entre ellas, las plantas salvajes son mucho más puras –y por lo tanto más puros sus aceites– que las plantas cultivadas.

Sin embargo, estas últimas pueden utilizarse sin dificultad siempre y cuando su crecimiento se realice en un marco natural (evitando productos químicos que puedan volverlas impuras para ser utilizadas como plantas curativas).

Existen dos métodos principales para extraer los aceites básicos de las plantas, pero es importante aclarar que ambos métodos son de muy difícil realización casera.

En general, los aromaterapeutas obtienen los aceites ya extraídos y, hoy en día, pueden conseguirse la mayoría de ellos en casas del ramo.

Los métodos indicados son:

1. Método de destilación por vapor
2. Método del estrujado

Durante el embarazo no se deben utilizar
aceites esenciales, pues los mismos pueden llegar
a causar severos trastornos de la piel
y del bienestar general.

Recordemos que en el embarazo se
tantes cambios hormonales por los
pueden llegar a ocasionar alteraciones
la vez que mareos, alteraciones del sueño,

Consejos para la adecuada conservación de los aceites

Si quieres que tus aceites conserven sus propiedades por más tiempo, presta atención a lo siguiente:

a Los aceites deben conservarse en frascos de vidrio.

b El vidrio de los frascos debe ser de color oscuro para evitar que penetre la luz.

c El ambiente en donde se conserve a los aceites debe ser oscuro y fresco.

d Las tapas deben cerrar en forma hermética para impedir que el aire pueda penetrar, deteriorando el aceite.

e Es conveniente adquirir frascos que posean en su extremo un gotero interno, a fin de no desperdiciar ninguna gota de aceite evitando derramamientos.

elección del aceite adecuado

De los cientos de aceites esenciales que existen en la actualidad, hay algunos cuyo uso es específico para cumplir con los objetivos planteados en este libro: relajar, armonizar, descontracturar. A continuación hallarás el nombre de cada aceite esencial y en qué casos se aprovechan mejor sus virtudes.

PACHULÍ

Actúa sobre la depresión y propicia la agudeza del ingenio y la elaboración de ideas. Es, a la vez, excelente cicatrizante y tónico nervioso.

MANZANILLA

Desde siempre ha sido considerada un remedio ideal para los nervios y se la utiliza en casos de insomnio y dolor de cabeza de origen nervioso, pero tiene también cualidades antidepresivas, antiinflamatorias y analgésicas.

SÁNDALO

Además de ser la base de perfumes más antigua que se conoce, este aceite tiene propiedades antisépticas a nivel urinario y pulmonar, además de mejorar la piel agrietada. Su nutriente más fuerte actúa sobre las consecuencias orgánicas que produce el estrés.

◎ LAVANDA

Es un aceite ampliamente utilizado por su poder analgésico, antidepresivo, antirreumático, antiséptico, cicatrizante, tónico nervioso, hipotensor y sedante. Además, ha dado excelentes resultados para mejorar el insomnio y la cefalea de origen nervioso.

◎ GERANIO

Además de su poder de equilibrar casi todas las funciones orgánicas, es un excelente remedio para problemas de la piel como el acné, la grasitud y la celulitis.

◎ ANGÉLICA

Los chinos utilizan esta especie para estimular la fertilidad y fortificar la vida espiritual. Actualmente su uso está extendido a otros aspectos como el de disminuir los efectos de la fatiga y la tensión nerviosa, y estimular la barrera inmunológica para prevenir resfríos y bronquitis.

◎ NEROLÍ

Este aceite se extrae del azahar y tiene un aroma exquisito. Es un relajante natural que equilibra el sistema nervioso, reduce las palpitaciones y mejora la piel agrietada y arrugada.

◎ INCIENSO

Tiene efecto sobre la piel envejecida y es eficaz para calmar la tos, el asma y el dolor de garganta. Su aroma impregna las ceremonias religiosas desde el fondo de la Antigüedad y convoca a la paz espiritual.

NARANJA (CHINA)
Es un equilibrante del sistema nervioso, es decir que seda pero promueve a la vez la actividad intelectual.

SALVIA
Antiséptico y antiinflamatorio, actúa sobre todo el organismo mejorando sus funciones vitales.

POMELO (TORONJA)
Esta fruta es energizante por excelencia y se recomienda su aceite en casos de agotamiento mental o físico.

BERGAMOTA
Es el aceite esencial contra la depresión por antonomasia y suele usarse en forma externa para movilizar el sistema muscular.

ROMERO
Revitalizante y energético, este aceite despierta los sentidos y mejora la respuesta física al estímulo.

JAZMÍN
Tiene poder antidepresivo, combate la ansiedad y mejora la respuesta sexual.

Principales usos de los aceites

A continuación enumeramos los principales usos de los aceites en la aromaterapia, en lo que tiene que ver específicamente con la relajación y la distensión.

1 masajes

2 baños

3 inhalaciones

4 máscaras

5 compresas

El punto número 1 (Masajes) ha sido
desarrollado en las páginas a color de este libro.
Por esa razón, brindaremos solamente
algunas definiciones para ir directamente
al punto siguiente.

Antes de comenzar con el desarrollo de cada uno de los puntos, lee atentamente la frase que sigue, pues es de suma importancia:

**Antes de aplicar un aceite esencial
es imprescindible
realizar una prueba cutánea.**

Algunas personas pueden ser alérgicas a determinados compuestos de los aceites básicos. Por lo tanto, antes de utilizarlos aplica una pequeña porción del mismo sobre la piel del interior del brazo o sobre la piel interior del codo.

Coloca una venda sobre el lugar y sostenla con una cinta adhesiva. Mantén la venda durante 24 horas —no laves la zona— y, transcurrido ese tiempo, retira la venda.

Si la zona de aplicación aparece con manchas rojas, puntos rojos o picazón, no debes utilizar ese aceite por ningún motivo.

Masajes

Los masajes son estimulantes de la circulación sanguínea y por lo tanto benefician y facilitan la penetración del aceite en la piel.

El masaje de cualquier parte del cuerpo debe hacerse con movimientos suaves, y fundamentalmente –para lograr un máximo de beneficio– en un ambiente que facilite la relajación.

Cada persona debe buscar el momento adecuado de su día para brindarse los masajes aromaterapéuticos.

Baños

Para que un baño con aceite aromático sea exitoso, debes mantener el ambiente libre de corrientes de aire. De esta forma, no sólo la piel absorberá el aceite, sino que también lo inhalarás a través del vapor que se desprende del agua caliente, a la que le has agregado el aceite.

Cuando se trata de baños, no debes aplicar el aceite directamente en el agua. Si lo haces, verás cómo el aceite queda flotando en la misma sin posibilidad de unión.

Para aprovechar al máximo el aceite, colócalo en un frasco con un poco de champú y agua tibia.

Bate enérgicamente la mezcla y luego incorpórala en el agua del baño.

Los baños estimulan y tonifican la piel
a la vez que relajan el sistema nervioso y proveen
un importante caudal de energía al organismo.

a Llena la bañera hasta sus tres cuartas partes con agua tibia.

b Introduce el aceite de la manera que se ha indicado anteriormente.

c Sumérgete dentro del agua de manera que todo el cuerpo quede cubierto.

d Cada tanto empápate el rostro y cuero cabelludo con el agua aceitada.

e Mientras dura el baño aprovecha a masajear bien el cuerpo.

f El baño debe durar diez minutos como mínimo, a fin de que el aceite penetre completamente.

Inhalaciones

Existen dos técnicas para realizar las inhalaciones, y ambas pueden ser utilizadas sin ninguna dificultad.

Técnica número 1

a Coloca el aceite elegido en una olla y cúbrelo con un poco de agua.

b Lleva la olla al fuego, el que debe ser moderado para que no salpique, y una vez que comience a desprender vapor, retírala y apaga el fuego.

c Toma una toalla limpia y cubre la cabeza con ella.

d Inclina el rostro sobre la olla y aspira el vapor.

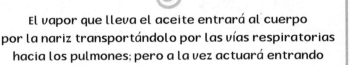

El vapor que lleva el aceite entrará al cuerpo por la nariz transportándolo por las vías respiratorias hacia los pulmones; pero a la vez actuará entrando a través de la piel del rostro.

Técnica número 2

a Coloca unas gotas de aceite en las palmas de tus manos y frótalas.

b Lleva enseguida las palmas hacia la nariz y aspira profundamente el aroma que desprende.

c Inhala varias veces siguiendo este procedimiento para que el aceite pueda penetrar más profundamente.

> Las inhalaciones limpian los senos paranasales y los bronquios congestionados.

Máscaras faciales

Antes que nada, te recomendamos que utilices siempre máscaras que respondan a tu tipo de cutis.

a Agrega a la base de la máscara que utilizas habitualmente unas gotas del aceite elegido, antes de aplicarla sobre el rostro.

b Aplica la máscara y déjala descansar el tiempo que indique el producto.

c Retírala como lo haces habitualmente.

Compresas

a Toma un paño suave y limpio, el que usarás exclusivamente para la realización de las compresas.

b Pon a calentar, en una olla, agua junto con el aceite elegido.

c Cuando el agua esté caliente, sumerge el paño, deja que se embeba bien del agua que contiene el aceite, retuércelo un poco para que no chorree y aplícalo en la zona que deseas relajar.

d Repite esta operación varias veces, sumergiendo el paño cada vez que se enfríe.

EL BIENESTAR ESTÁ
en tus manos

No pierdas la oportunidad

Con la información que acabamos de brindarte en este capítulo sobre el maravilloso poder de la aromaterapia y las virtudes increíbles de los aceites esenciales tienes en tus manos la posibilidad de llevar el bienestar a tu vida y a la de tu pareja cada vez que lo desees o lo consideres conveniente.

La aplicación de los aceites esenciales es sumamente sencilla y puedes recurrir a esta técnica no sólo en el caso de hacer un masaje corporal completo a tu pareja, sino en caso de hacer un pequeño, suave y breve masaje facial, o en alguna zona del cuerpo que tú o él noten tensa, dolorida o contracturada.

La idea es que el masaje llegue a tu vida para quedarse y que no sea un hecho excepcional sino parte de tus actividades placenteras.

A medida que lo vayas practicando, te darás cuenta de cuántos beneficios aporta, tanto a nivel físico como a nivel emocional y espiritual.

Te lo garantizamos: tú y tu pareja comenzarán a sentirse más vigorosos y plenos que nunca, pues con el masaje realizado en forma frecuente los músculos se distienden y se tonifican, a la vez que se activa la circulación sanguínea de todo el cuerpo.

La importancia de la relajación

Los aceites son los aliados incondicionales del masaje a la hora de alcanzar su objetivo primordial: relajar. Pero tu actitud y la de tu pareja también son sumamente importantes en este sentido.

Los aceites, además de penetrar en la piel, liberan su aroma al entrar en contacto con el calor corporal y este aroma es el que, al percibirse, despierta los sentidos y prepara tanto a quien da como a quien recibe el masaje para la relajación.

Si al hacer o recibir el masaje estás tensa o pensando en lo que tienes que hacer luego no obtendrás el resultado esperado. Deja que el aroma del aceite te conecte directamente con lo que estás haciendo y libera tu mente de cualquier clase de pensamiento. El masaje es pura sensación y la racionalidad no tiene lugar en él.

Palabras finales

Ya sabes que para que una pareja perdure es tan importante dar como recibir amor. Y el amor –también lo sabes– tiene múltiples formas de expresarse. De ti depende que el masaje se convierta en un nuevo canal de comunicación con tu pareja, en una nueva forma de expresar tus sentimientos.

¡Que tengas mucha suerte!

ÍNDICE